PHOENIX RISING

Werner Forman

PHOENIX RISING

The United Arab Emirates
Past, Present & Future

Text by Michael Asher
Design by Barney Wan

THE HARVILL PRESS
LONDON

First published in Great Britain 1996 by
The Harvill Press
84 Thornhill Road
London N1 1RD

A CIP catalogue record for this title is available from the British Library

ISBN 1 86046 155 7

Typeset in Spectrum at The Libanus Press, Marlborough, Wiltshire
Printed and bound in Great Britain by Butler & Tanner, Frome and London

CONTENTS

LEFT: Brass coffee-pot. 'Hornbill-spouted' pots like this *dallah* were once to be found in every Arab house or tent in the Emirates. Fashioned in brass or copper, many were imported from Nezwa or Ibri in Oman. (*al-'Ain Museum*)

TITLE PAGE: The Hajar mountains seen from the west. Presenting a forbidding aspect of sawblade edges, these hills are the oldest mountain range in eastern Arabia. The Hajar chain began to form twenty million years ago when the peninsula's continental shelf was driven against the rugged substrata of Iran.

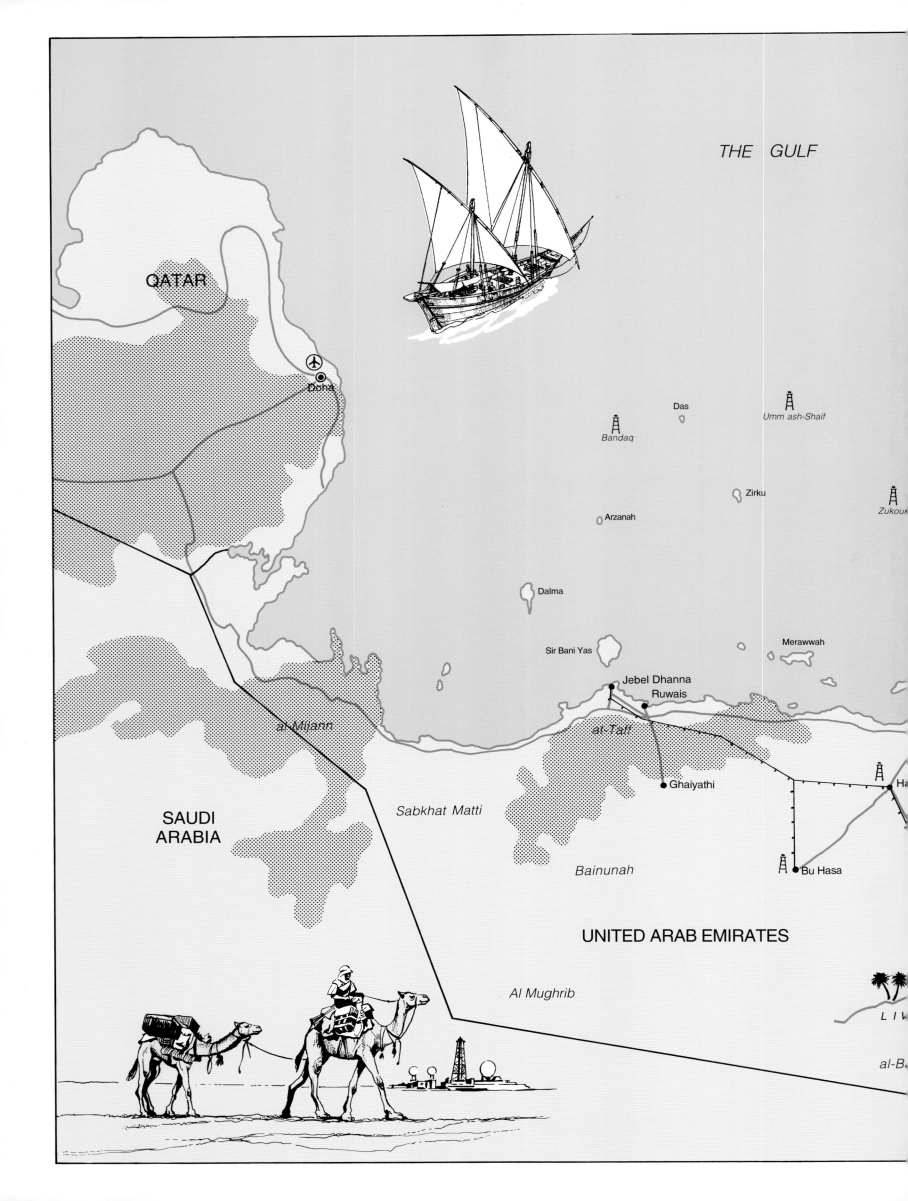

THE GULF

QATAR

Doha

Das

Umm ash-Shaif

Bandaq

Zirku

Zukou

Arzanah

Dalma

Merawwah

Sir Bani Yas

Jebel Dhanna
Ruwais

al-Milann

al-Taff

H

SAUDI
ARABIA

Sabkhat Matti

Ghaiyathi

Bu Hasa

Bainunah

UNITED ARAB EMIRATES

Al Mughrib

L I V

al-B

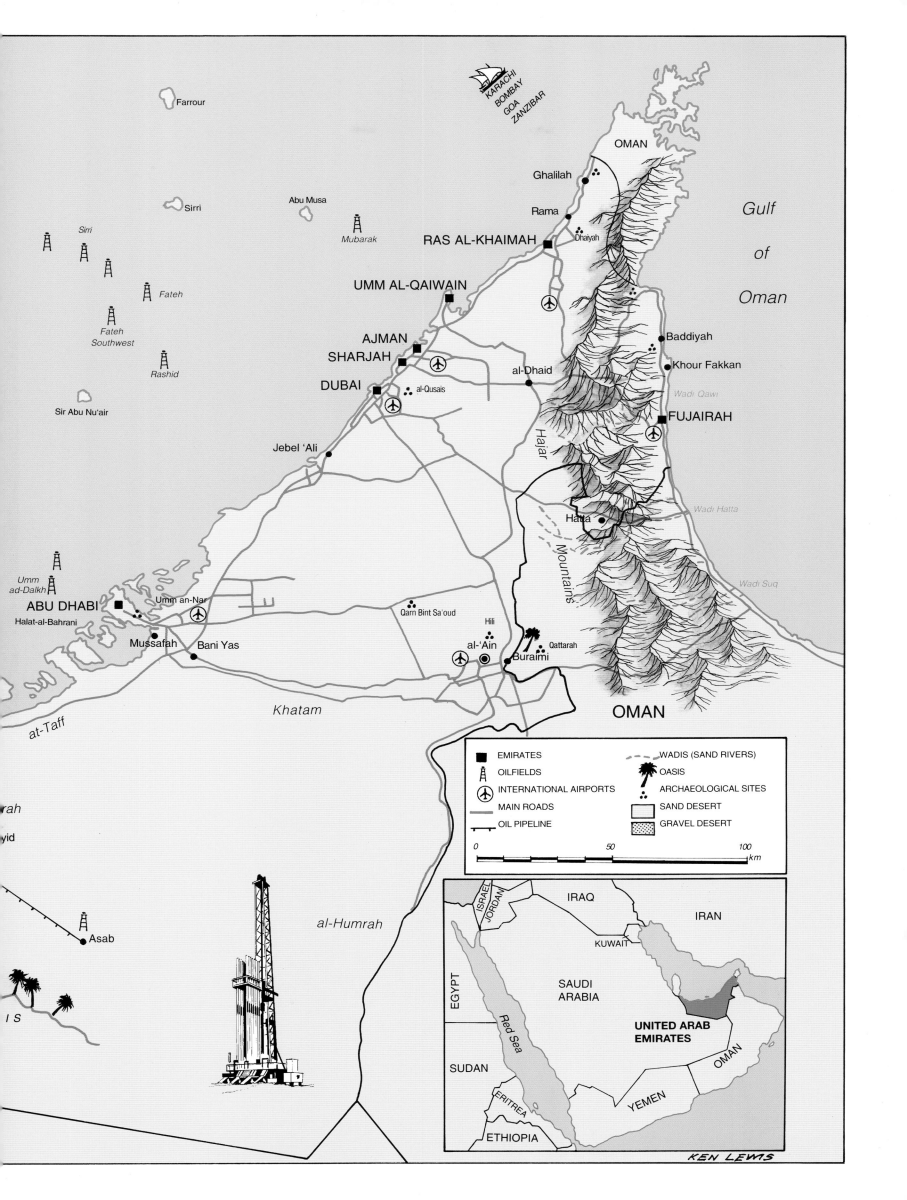

Farrour

Sirri
Sirri

Abu Musa

Fateh

Mubarak

Fateh Southwest

Rashid

Sir Abu Nu'air

Umm ad-Dalkh

ABU DHABI

Halat-al-Bahrani

Umm an-Nar

Mussafah   Bani Yas

at-Taff

Khatam

rah

yid

Asab

I S

al-Humrah

Karachi
Bombay
Goa
Zanzibar

OMAN

Ghalilah

Rama

Dhaiyah

RAS AL-KHAIMAH

UMM AL-QAIWAIN

AJMAN

SHARJAH

DUBAI

al-Qusais

Jebel 'Ali

al-Dhaid

Baddiyah

Khour Fakkan

Wadi Qawi

FUJAIRAH

Hajar

Hatta

Wadi Hatta

Mountains

Wadi Suq

Qarn Bint Sa'oud

Hili

al-'Ain

Buraimi

Qattarah

OMAN

Gulf

of

Oman

	EMIRATES		WADIS (SAND RIVERS)
	OILFIELDS		OASIS
	INTERNATIONAL AIRPORTS		ARCHAEOLOGICAL SITES
	MAIN ROADS		SAND DESERT
	OIL PIPELINE		GRAVEL DESERT

0   50   100
                                              km

ISRAEL
JORDAN

IRAQ

IRAN

KUWAIT

EGYPT

SAUDI ARABIA

Red Sea

UNITED ARAB EMIRATES

SUDAN

ERITREA

OMAN

YEMEN

ETHIOPIA

KEN LEWIS

INTRODUCTION

Michael Asher

From high above, the coast is a ragged seam of surf along ochre beaches – to the west a web of reefs and islands basking in iridescent waters, to the east an austere world of dunes and sand bars bounded only by the naked hills. The land and its people have been fashioned by these potent forces – the desert, the mountains, and the sea. At this altitude the works of man are stains of light and shade against the infinity of the landscape, but draw closer and they assume a more commanding scope – six-lane highways with glittering streams of motorcars, dream cities of ivory-white and crystal glass rising like spectres out of the waves. From Abu Dhabi island, with its palm trees and palaces, the shore curves inwards through glittering salt flats and lagoons for 120 kilometres, to be fractured again by the creek and boulevards of Dubai. To the north, the minarets of Sharjah, Ajman and Umm al-Qaiwain flash from inlets and sand spits; at Ras al-Khaimah majestic cliffs rise sheer from the ocean, and beyond the Hajar mountains lies Fujairah. These are the seven cities which – with their hinterlands – form the United Arab Emirates, the federation of independent states which in little more than twenty-five years has bloomed from near poverty into one of the richest countries on earth.

That such cities have sprung up in only a quarter of a century is a remarkable tribute to the versatile character of the region's people. When oil exploration first started here in the late 1940s, there was no electricity, no plumbing or telephone system, not a single public hospital or modern school, no bridges, no deep-water harbour, no metalled roads, no more than a handful of cars, and scarcely a building more impressive than the crumbling coral stone and gypsum forts and the ancient watchtowers of Abu Dhabi and Dubai. Where now monumental skyscrapers loom over spacious avenues, where cascades of water are flaunted with opulent abandon, and where acres of imported shrubs burgeon into green upon the desert shore, stood drowsy settlements of reed, coral and mud houses, sweltering on inlets and sand banks in the most ferocious of summer climes.

Life on the Trucial Coast – as the region was then called – was one of considerable hardship. In the towns, fresh water was available only from wells, and had to be hauled to the surface by hand, or even brought in barrels from neighbouring islands by dhow. Tribesmen would harvest the fickle winter rains by stretching a sail with a hole in its centre between two poles, and in the *humid* summers, would tap the cooling winds by the skilful use of wind-towers made of sacking or cotton cloth. On the mountain terraces subsistence farmers eked out a bitter existence, hand-watering palm groves and millet from goatskins, and in the deserts beyond the Bedouin might live for months on only camels' milk, in some places obtaining their water by squeezing the dew from rags slung on thorn bushes overnight. When the leanness of their lives drove them over the edge of survival, Bedouin raiders would appear ominously on the marches of the cultivated land, pillaging livestock and date gardens. The many ruined forts and watchtowers still seen today in almost every part of the country bear mute testimony to its troubled past.

Although the greater settlements of the Emirates have traditionally looked out to the sea, it is the desert which has stamped the character of the region's people most clearly. The sands of the vast Empty Quarter – *Rub 'al-Khali* – roll up to the very shores of the Gulf, varying in texture from the

Aerial view of Dubai and its creek, 1950. *Ronald Codrai*

Aerial view of Abu Dubi and its fort, 1950. *Ronald Codrai*

undulating red steppe of the coastal foreland, to the great jelly-mould sand mountains of the interior. No human being could live for long inside the Empty Quarter during the summer months, when the air temperature reaches 50°C in the shade, and the surface of the sand is fired to a formidable 80°C.

In these sands living organisms were, over time, obliged to learn the tricks of moisture conservation to survive. In much of the Empty Quarter only six species of hardy shrub prevailed, the most abundant among them being calligonum, a brush-like sedge whose waxy bark prevented water-loss, and whose roots were able to absorb rainwater with efficient speed. The seeds of such plants might hibernate in the sand for years, awaiting only a downpour before erupting into brilliant bloom. They provided a refuge for scorpions, skinks, spiders, darkling beetles, sand vipers and toad-headed lizards, and to mammals such as Cheeseman's gerbil, Ruppell's sand fox, and the Cape hare — none of which ever needed to drink water in their entire lives. The desert was also the domain of the Arabian oryx — the great antelope which was able to locate desert vegetation by its acute sense of smell and migrate 100 kilometres in a night.

The few Bedouin families courageous enough to venture to the interior during the cooler times were obliged to make equally drastic adaptations to their social organization, for in the Empty Quarter rain fell only locally, and those who would live there had to be mobile enough to reach the distant pastures wherever it had rained. Everything they owned had to be light and manageable enough to hoist on to a camel's back. Their camel herds were survival machines, converting the sparse grazing into the milk that was for the Bedouin both food and drink. To travel in the terrible *Rub 'al-Khali* with the herds was, they said, to travel in relative abundance: to journey there alone was to gamble with death.

It is amid the harsh deserts of the Empty Quarter that the modern history of the United Arab Emirates begins. In the early fifteenth or sixteenth centuries members of a Bedouin tribe called the Bani Yas occupied the Liwa oasis — a sweeping crescent of palm groves amid rippling dunes 100 kilometres south of the coast. There, they began to cultivate the date palm, the 'prince of trees' — a very different existence from the wandering life they had formerly enjoyed. The trees required constant attention: palm-fibre shields to prevent sand-drift, careful pruning to encourage growth, hand-pollination from male to female trees in the spring, and — most arduous of all — daily watering by hand until the roots of the young saplings had groped to the water-table. In return, almost every part of the tree produced something that was of use – the trunk provided construction beams, and the fronds became mats, beds, fishing canoes, fences, windbreaks, water vessels, huts and traditional dwellings; the leaves could be worked into fans, baskets, bags and food trays, the bast into ropes and the stuffing for cushions, mattresses, saddles and roofing-material – even the date stones could be fed to goats. The value of such by-products paled into insignificance, however, beside that of the date itself, which remained the major source of nourishment in the region until recent times.

Soon, these former Bedouin had abandoned the nomad life almost entirely and given themselves up to rearing date trees. In 1761, a group of them ventured north, eventually founding a village on an island off the coast which they named Abu Dhabi, "The Place of the Gazelle". The moment was opportune, for the Gulf then stood on the brink of a worldwide boom in the demand for pearls, which had been harvested off these shores for at least six thousand years. The Bani Yas quickly went into the pearling business, buying pearling boats communally and sharing out the profits among the tribe. By the end of the eighteenth century they were wealthy enough to build themselves houses in Abu Dhabi, and their descendants prospered. A hundred years later the Trucial Coast's pearling fleet consisted of more than 1200 boats, employed more than 22,000 men – almost the entire adult male population of the region – and valued its trade at a then staggering 1.5 million pounds.

By the mid 1800s, the al-Bu Falah family, who had emerged as the paramount sheikhs of Abu Dhabi, had begun to extend their influence in the deserts to the east, acquiring control of the al-'Ain – Buraimi oasis, famous for its vegetable gardens and luxuriant palm groves. Divided into a number of villages, the oasis was dominated by two tribes, one, the Dhawahir, owing fealty to the Sheikh of Abu Dhabi, and the second, the Na'im – a branch of which still rules the small Emirate of

A *quityah* returning from the Indian Ocean, 1950s. *Ronald Codrai*

Ajman on the coast – to the Sultan of Oman. By acting as protectors to their Dhawahir vassals, the al-Bu Falah skilfully made use of traditional tensions between the tribes to consolidate their authority and to acquire palm groves and gardens there. Many such gardens were very ancient, for a sophisticated water-system, the *aflaaj*, (sing. *falaj*) had been in place at al-'Ain since before the time of Solomon. A *falaj* consisted of a series of vertical air shafts bored into the earth, connected by a horizontal conduit averaging about seven kilometres in length. Since the oasis lay in a depression, water would be sucked down the conduit from the surrounding highlands by the force of gravity, and transferred into the cultivated area through a web of feeder channels. The only human energy necessary was that required to open and close such channels with stones. Traditionally, about twelve *aflaaj* operated in the al-'Ain–Buraimi area, though by the end of the 1960s only seven remained in use.

In 1833 a breakaway group of the Bani Yas of Abu Dhabi – the al-Bu Falasa – moved up the coast and settled on the creek at Dubai. From then on the two branches of the family lived in competition: while Abu Dhabi continued to take its character from the boundless desert behind it, drawing support from Bedouin tribes such as the Manasir, Dubai turned outwards to the sea, becoming a powerful generator of trade. Its ships – *baghlahs*, *qutiyahs*, *sambuks* and *booms* – were soon tacking across the Gulf to Persia, and – laden with coffee, rice, sugar, cotton cloth and mangrove poles – riding the monsoon winds home from Zanzibar and Bombay. By the end of the nineteenth century, while Abu Dhabi was still little more than a village and a market centred around the Sheikh's fort, Dubai had become the leading port on the Lower Gulf – a cosmopolitan town with a population of 20,000, where Farsi, Baluchi and Hindi were as likely to be heard in the market as Arabic. Though Abu Dhabi is today itself a noble city of some 500,000 souls, these contrasts in perspective and character – commerce versus terrestrial power: the desert versus the sea – remain largely unchanged.

The commercial success of the al-Bu Falashah in Dubai brought them into rivalry with the coast's other powerful trading family, the Qawasim, whose chief port, Sharjah, lay only a few kilometres further along the coast, and who also ruled Ras al-Khaimah, and held sway over the sheikhs of Umm al-Qaiwain. They had been seafarers for generations, and regarded the waters of the Lower Gulf much as the Bani Yas regarded their deserts. Any vessels entering this

The Corniche Abu Dhabi, 1948. *Wilfred Thesiger*

region did so at their peril, for the Qawasim viewed them with the same cupidity with which Bedouin raiders saw a fat caravan traversing their territory. Qasimi vessels so far irritated the British with attacks on ships under their protection, that in the early nineteenth century the Royal Navy several times bombarded their ports, eventually sinking the Qasimi fleet as it lay in the creek of Ras al-Khaimah. There was, of course, more behind British truculence than the threat to shipping.

Their goal was to establish dominance over the region and to exclude rival powers from influence there. In 1820, following the virtual destruction of the Qasimi flotilla, they forced the sheikhs of six of the present-day Emirates, (Fujairah was not recognized until 1952), to sign agreements giving them control over the area's defence and foreign policy, but absolving them from responsibility in internal affairs. In time-honoured Imperial fashion, the British tacitly encouraged internal squabbles in order to keep the area weak and disunited. The power of the Qawasim waned after the curtailment of their sea-faring activities, and though their port of Sharjah remained of consequence until the turn of the next century, their ascendancy was gradually eclipsed by that of the Bani Yas, and Sharjah's status ultimately inherited by Dubai.

The hinterland of the Qawasim regions differed from that of the desert-oriented Bani Yas, in that it included the Hajar mountains, a barren, igneous mass of fractured peaks and soaring vertical valleys, which filled the horizons only a few dozen kilometres to the east. It was the Hajar massif that more than anything else had determined the arid nature of the land, for the mountains acted as a moisture-trap, milking the monsoon wind before it could jettison its liquid on the desert plains beyond. In summer, when rough peaks gashed the clouds, rains burst upon the uplands, tumbling down the ravines and *wadis* until the spates were soaked up by the sands, providing ground water for the oasis of al-'Ain and as far west as Dubai.

An *'abra* (ferry boat) against a background of wind-towers on the Dubai waterfront, 1948. *Ronald Codrai*

13

A desert homestead, 1948. *Wilfred Thesiger*

This was a world away from the deserts of the interior. Oleanders with pink and white flowers, and euphorbia trees like ornate candelabras flourished in the highlands as they did nowhere else in the country, and leopards might be glimpsed in the high valleys, stalking *tahr* — an endemic species of mountain goat. Yet it was no garden of Eden. On the western, rain-shadow side the valleys were mostly so barren that no topsoil remained. In the few spots where cultivation was possible the farming tribes were obliged to build and maintain water-terraces to prevent the occasional floods from leaching away the vital soil. Only on the eastern side — facing the Gulf of Oman — were perennial streams to be found, and here, at the foot of the mountain wall, the small Sheikhdom of Fujairah flourished amid its jungles of palms — a solitary bloom severed from easy land contact with the other centres of power by the tortuous passes of the Hajar mountains.

In the eighteenth century, a sheikh named Abdallah bin Muhammad brought together the fractious, feuding clans of the Sharqiyyin — the dominant mountain tribe of the area — to defend their valleys against incursions from the west. His descendants have ruled Fujairah ever since. Looking as much to Oman as to the eastern Emirates, the Sheikhdom developed its own unique character. Here, the lumbering ox cocked a snook at the plains-adapted camel, and bull-fighting developed as a sport as it did nowhere else in the region. Here the tribes, more fortunate in their access to water, practised spring-fed agriculture, and built hamlets of mud and stone. These permanently settled farmers occupied the opposite end of the spectrum from the ultra-mobile Bedouin of the Empty Quarter.

While the social structure of each of the seven Trucial states varied according to the terrain — with nomads, and oasis-farmers preponderant in the desert areas, and semi-nomads and settled mountain-farmers more numerous in those abutting the hills — these groups had never been static. Many farming clans had at one time been camel-breeding Bedouin who had settled on agricultural land, just as many Bedouin tribes had experienced the life of cultivators at some period in the past. The limited resources of this parched landscape meant that every family must include individuals who were jacks of all trades rather than masters of one.

Both farmers and herders sought work in the pearling fleets in the summer, and in times of plenty might take root in town for several years. Until the present generation it was not at all unusual to find tribesmen who were as well-versed in harvesting date palms as they were skilled in diving

14

for pearls, equally at home whether rearing camels or navigating a *sambuk* on the high seas. It was this readiness of the ordinary tribesman to turn his hand to anything — his characteristic versatility, shrewdness in commerce, adventurous spirit, tolerance, patience and flexibility — which later enabled him to adapt so readily to far-reaching changes, and yet preserve his values intact.

The sea has provided a common denominator for all the Emirates since earliest times. Hemmed in by desert and mountain, it was to the ocean that the coastal peoples looked for contact with the outside world. More than five thousand years ago, tribes already settled on the islands and creeks of these shores were trading with the civilization of the Indus, and providing revictualling-stations for ships bound for the cities of Mesopotamia. Such centres were not only trading entrepots, but also distribution posts for raw materials such as copper, diorite and chlorite, to the affluent cities of ancient Sumer.

What is today the United Arab Emirates may then have been the famous country of Magan, noted in Mesopotamian texts as one of its three major suppliers of copper and useful stones. The scores of beehive tombs found at Jebel Hafit — a lone hogsback of sedimentary rock towering over al-'Ain oasis — and nearby at Qarn Bint Sa'oud, may well have belonged to this copper-smelting culture. Among their ruins have been discovered fragments of a cup, and a bracelet made of an alloy of copper and arsenic typical of primitive copper industries of that time. The copper-people mined the rich seam of ore running through the mountains around al-'Ain, digging it out with sharp stones, and smelting the crushed rock in a charcoal furnace which consisted of little more than a hole in the ground. Since a phenomenal heat of 1200° C was required to separate the copper from its lode, enormous quantities of timber for charcoal were needed, and had the copper-smelters remained in one place the scanty vegetation would quickly have been destroyed. Instead, they were probably nomadic, wandering the mountains with donkeys, goats and sheep, halting for a while wherever they found abundant wood. The final product — the copper ingots — were transported to the coast and sold to Mesopotamian merchants at trading centres such as Umm an-Nar island — near present-day Abu Dhabi.

In 2700 BC, Umm an-Nar was a thriving port of stone-built houses whose exteriors were finished

Launching a dhow, 1948. *Wilfred Thesiger*

with mud-brick of a type characteristic of Mesopotamian buildings of the period. Several tombs found at Umm an-Nar – circular structures faced with limestone blocks – also reveal a Mesopotamian influence. They were collective graves, incorporating a number of chambers which contained grave goods of fine chlorite pottery. Similar buildings have been discovered in many sites in the Emirates, the most exceptional being the pillbox-shaped tombs at Hili, near al-'Ain, decorated with unique relief carvings of human figures and animals. The tomb builders of Hili evidently lived in an era of great prosperity, for their bones display physiques of remarkable robustness, and their middens have revealed that they lived on a diet more varied and nutritious than that of their successors in the early twentieth century. Before 2000 BC, indeed, the region that was to become the Emirates was probably more affluent than at any period up to the last twenty-five years, and since then has bloomed and declined several times. Like the legendary phoenix, civilization here has periodically been consumed by the ashes, only to rise again in the fullness of time.

The pearling boom of the nineteenth century was the motive force behind just such a renascence. Droves of nomadic Bedouin and farmers alike poured into the coastal towns during the season to share in the stupendous profits to be made on the pearling ships. Yet despite such bounty, they found life aboard them no easy option. The vessel might lie off shore for four months on end, and there was no shade or shelter on deck from the blasting sun. The divers worked from an hour after dawn till sunset on empty stomachs, sustained only by gulps of bitter coffee, making about sixty dives in a day, each of about a minute's duration. Lashed to his haulers, the diver would plummet to the seabed weighted by a boulder attached to his foot. His ears blocked with wax, his nose sealed with a bone peg, his fingers tipped with leather caps, and wearing a ragged cotton shirt against the stings of jellyfish, he would fill a basket with a dozen oysters before his air expired, tugging sharply on the rope as a signal to haul him up. When the limpid waters turned opaque near sundown, he was hoisted on board to break his fast with fish, rice, coffee and dates – his only meal of the day. Not until first light the following morning would the oysters be sliced open to reveal the value of the catch. Only the largest pearls were of sufficient quality to be sold individually. Most were sold in quantity to pearl merchants – many of them from India – who either visited the fleet while it was still on the oyster beds, or met the vessels when they returned to port *en masse*. No pearling boat was permitted to return to its home base alone, to prevent any individual owner from cornering the market.

The pearl trade's weakness lay in its dependence on the vagaries of fashion. In the Victorian era, a string of pearls had been not only a symbol of wealth but an exotic souvenir of the mysteries of the east. In the early decades of the twentieth century, however, war and economic recession in the West led to a gradual downturn. Year by year the fleets grew smaller, and nomads and farmers returned to their hills and deserts. Many families left the Trucial Coast entirely for more affluent regions nearby, leading to a steep fall in population between 1900 and 1950. The Bedouin, beset by the consequent slump in the value of camels, resorted once again to raiding. In 1931 alone, Bedouin of the 'Awamir – a tribe which customarily wintered in the Empty Quarter – were reported to be harrying the outskirts of Sharjah, Ras al-Khaimah, and Dubai, and pillaging date gardens in Umm al-Qaiwain. In the same year they attacked a caravan from Fujairah, only to be driven off by the resolute townsmen who killed three and captured a fourth. The crisis slowly worsened, however, and all hope of recovery was shattered when, in the late 1930s, it became known that the Japanese had invented the cultured pearl. In 1946 the Indian government outlawed any further import of natural pearls from the Gulf. The last pearling fleet of any size put into Dubai in 1949.

Yet long before the Indian embargo, new winds were blowing across the coast, heralding changes which, within a single generation, would transform this poverty-stricken land where every piece of bread and gulp of water was dearly earned, to a country that was wealthy beyond the most fabulous of the 1001 tales of the *Arabian Nights*. Even as the ingenious Japanese were developing their home-bred pearl, crude oil was already being pumped from rich fields in nearby Bahrein. By the late 1930s, Western oil companies had begun to turn their hungry gaze to the potentially oil-rich hinterlands and waters of the Trucial Coast. Dubai signed its first concession for

Sheikh Rashid, with his daughter on his lap, attended by retainers, in the early 1950s. Sheikh Rashid was the elder son of the then ruler, Sheikh Sa'id, who later became ruler of Dubai and Vice-President of the UAE. *Ronald Codrai*

oil exploration in 1937, and Abu Dhabi two years later, in 1939. These concessions inevitably fostered conflict. Suddenly aware of the value of their land, the al-Bu Falah (now the al-Nahyan) of Abu Dhabi, and the al-Maktoum — by now the paramount sheikhs of Dubai — began to dispute the demarcation of their respective borders. In 1945 raids and skirmishes between their Bedouin retainers culminated in a desperate war between Shakhbout bin Sultan al Nahyan, Ruler of Abu Dhabi, and Sa'id al Maktoum, Ruler of Dubai.

Though oil wells were spudded-in at Ras as Sadr in 1950 and at Bab One, Jebel Ali and others in 1953, it was to be another decade before the Trucial Coast saw its first oil export. In 1962, after years of seismic surveys, fruitless drilling and endless negotiation, a British tanker finally weighed anchor at Das Island — 160 kilometres off Abu Dhabi — with the first 50,000 barrels of local crude. Oil was struck at the Fateh field off Dubai in 1966, and at Sharjah's Mubarak field in 1972. Four years later gas was discovered in non-commercial quantities off Umm al-Qaiwain, and Ras al-Khaimah's offshore Saleh field went into production in 1984. Neither in tiny Ajman — 279 square kilometres — nor in Fujairah have traces of petroleum yet been found. By 1981, the Emirates was exporting 73 million tons of crude oil annually, a third each to Europe, Japan, and the United States. By 1991, production was stabilized at 2.3 million barrels a day, and the value of oil exports calculated at more than 13 billion dollars per year.

Such a sum is perhaps as inconceivable to us now as it would have been to the young Sheikh Zayed bin Sultan — younger brother of the Ruler of Abu Dhabi — when he was appointed governor of the Sheikhdom's villages in al-'Ain in 1946. Born in a drafty fortress in the oasis to a family made virtually penniless by the collapse of the pearl trade, Zayed received only a basic education, and grew up in a world without roads, schools, hospitals, motorcars or electric light. Yet while still in his twenties his sagacity and sense of justice had already gained him a reputation among the desert tribes, who also admired him for his ability to live as they did. The explorer Wilfred Thesiger, who first met Zayed at al-'Ain in 1948, wrote: "he had a great reputation among the Bedou. They liked him for his easy,

H H Sheikh Zayed bin Sultan al-Nahyan, near Muwaiqih, 1950. *Wilfred Thesiger*

informal ways and his friendliness, and they respected his force of character, his shrewdness, and his physical strength. They said admiringly, 'Zayed is a (Bedui). He knows about camels, can ride like one of us, can shoot, and knows how to fight.'"

Zayed's qualities as an arbitrator were soon to be severely tested, when in 1952 Saudi-Arabian troops occupied part of the al 'Ain–Buraimi oasis, to which the Saudi Royal family had long laid claim. It took three years of negotiation – and eventually the backing of the British-officered Trucial Oman Scouts – before they were obliged to withdraw. Zayed's reputation enlarged manifold following the Buraimi crisis, while his elder brother, Shakhbout – Ruler of Abu Dhabi – found it increasingly difficult to deal with the new realities of oil wealth. In 1966, the al-Nahyan family chose Zayed to replace him as Ruler, only just in time to deal with the sensational news that in 1971 the British would be pulling out. With customary resolve, Abu Dhabi's new Ruler rose to the challenge. His goal was to bring about a federation between the independent-minded Sheikhdoms of the Trucial Coast which had lived in conflict for centuries – to forge from these individualistic city states a new, independent nation. It was to his good fortune that the Ruler of Dubai – Sheikh Rashid bin Sa'id al-Maktoum – was a man who shared his vision of the future, and who was equally willing to discard the antagonism of the past. They agreed that the new state would be governed by a Supreme Council consisting of the Rulers of all seven Emirates, with Zayed as President and Rashid as Vice-President and Prime Minister. On 2 December 1971, the green, black and white banner of the United Arab Emirates fluttered over the towns of the lower Gulf for the first time.

The union proved astonishingly successful. In the following twenty-five years, the quasi-medieval conditions of the Emirates were to undergo a metamorphosis so profound that any less adaptable people would have been utterly destroyed by it. Within two decades towns of coral houses and palm-frond huts had flowered into space-age cities of fine villas and apartment blocks; a transport system still incorporating the camel and the donkey had been replaced by 345,000 motor-vehicles and 2700 kilometres of metalled road; sand-locked harbours had been developed into fourteen state-of-the-art ports, including, at Dubai, the world's largest dry dock, with the Jebel 'Ali Free Zone becoming the manufacturing hub of the Gulf, the airfield at Sharjah having been exchanged for no less than six international airports. In the same twenty years, the traditional Arab remedy of 'burning' with hot irons to cure almost any ill had been superseded by forty-two custom-built hospitals, some of them with facilities for kidney transplants and open-heart surgery, and a national health service which covered even the most inaccessible hamlets of the Hajar mountains; traditional Islamic retreats in which students had written Quranic verses on the shoulder-blades of cows for lack of paper, had been supplanted by more than 700 modern schools and a national university, catering to almost half a million students. Even the barren landscape in which tribesmen had struggled for so many generations had been transformed in places into luxuriant gardens by massive infusions of desalinated water from the sea; vast areas which had once been desert had been planted with 60 million new trees, thousands of new farms had been established, and more than 100,000 hectares of virgin land had been turned under the plough.

Superlative might be added to superlative in describing the process by which the poorest of countries has been converted, within one generation, into a nation enjoying one of the highest standards of living on earth. Yet the crucial measure of success lies not in material things, but in the hearts and minds of its people. Not only has the United Arab Emirates remained the most stable country in the Middle East, but its citizens have performed the near miraculous task of balancing the impulse for change against the need for continuity with the past. This is perfectly symbolized in the architecture of the great cities of Abu Dhabi and Dubai, where inspiring modern buildings have been constructed to the most *avante-garde* of conceptions, and yet have still managed to maintain the character and spirit of Arab tradition. So it is with the people of the Emirates: it might be that a long history of ascent and decline has seasoned them well against the pitfalls of sudden change, for they remain as hospitable and unassuming in great wealth as they were in misfortune, preserving their sense of identity and their cultural traditions intact. No one knows what lies in the future, but the achievements of the United Arab Emirates over the past quarter-century remain an object lesson in what can be attained through adaptability, wise leadership, and an open-minded attitude to the world.

It is the triumph of Werner Forman to have expressed this sense of change and continuity so perfectly in his photographs. Few artists, perhaps, could have shown such feeling and such precision over so varied a range of themes. Whether his pictures portray a radar station in the sands, prehistoric grave-goods, a traditional silver necklace, or shipwrights building a dhow, he displays a rare ability to convey the essence of his subject. We see through his eyes that the colours of the sunset reflected in the glass of a tower block can be as fascinating as the colours in the desert sands: the lights on a desert highway at night as beautiful as a string of pearls. He skilfully avoids the trap of sentimentalism, while presenting us with images which are vivacious and alive. The achievements of the present, like the glories of the past, are imparted with subtle grace rather than dogmatic insistence. The picture of little girl in her classroom – totally absorbed in her drawing – for instance, says far more for the success of the education system than any official snap of pupils sitting rigidly at desks in military style. Werner Forman's photographs provide a comprehensive view of the United Arab Emirates from the earliest times to the present, balancing the traditional and the contemporary with consistent excellence. These images represent not only a fitting tribute to this nation's first twenty-five years by one of our foremost photographers, but also stand alone as the great attainment of a man with a tireless interest in the beauty of the world.

PAST, PRESENT AND FUTURE

Werner Forman

In the following ten pages I try to give less a preface than a preview of what is to follow. It is in the contrast of these images that we may glimpse the well-hidden face of this country's past, and possibly begin to project the hectic flux of the present onto the otherwise blank page of the future.

The reader may be surprised to find that every section of this book introduced with the title *Past, Present and Future*. History in general, and the history of the Emirates in particular, cannot be conveniently divided into tidy periods. The changes have been and still are proceeding so rapidly that any attempt to represent, or even define the present becomes pointless. To arrange the material of this book into discrete sections by subject matter proves equally vain.

The first of the four sections concentrates on early societies in the Emirates and the artifacts found buried in the sand at the sites of early settlements. The second section depicts the desert and its counterpart, the oases. The oasis societies grew, and have thrived, by virtue of their man-made irrigation systems. The subject of irrigation is thus clearly appropriate for this section, but archae-ological research has found that this *aflaaj* system of irrigation, still employed, has been in use for roughly three thousand years, giving it a valid place in the first section on early societies too. Simultaneously, the photograph in the final section of a water-supply plant expected to be fully operational at the time of publication, and thus straddling more than three thousand years of water management, points to the unwieldiness of every neat past–present–future division This is only one of many instances where the subject matter of one section spills over into the territory of another.

The third part, dealing with traditional ways of life, crafts and trade by sea and land, is rooted both in early times and in the very latest additions to the townscapes of the Emirates. Trading between this part of the Gulf and distant empires has been intense since antiquity, while on a local level there have always been links with the remotest, most inaccessible parts of the Emirates. The final section of the book tries to give an overview of the most recent developments in the country, hinting at things that may one day come to be the Emirates' present.

RIGHT: A young woman wearing a *burqa*. The face mask, like the later introduced veil, is part of a traditional attitude towards the appearance of women in public; it is not obligatory in Islamic doctrine, which prescribes only modesty of dress for both men and women. Mask and veil have another function in desert conditions worldwide, as both sexes dress for the greatest protection, keeping exposure to sand and sun to a minimum. The mask shown here, then, is worn as protection both against unwanted attention and against the elements. A combination of function and elegance, this Arabian addition to women's attire belongs now largely to the past. (*Ras al-Khaimah Museum*)

LEFT: Bone inlay figure, probably camel bone, from Asimah grave 24, first to second century AD. This bone tablet, described as 'furniture inlay', has a distinctive comb-like appearance. The carving shows the torso of a male figure, whether human, semi-divine or divine cannot be ascertained. Little attention has been paid to the figure's unusual stance, partly, perhaps, because of damage which has left a considerable part of the left arm missing. But there cannot be any doubt that the gesture, arms raised, palms turned outwards, is of great antiquity. Egyptian reliefs more than four thousand years old show people in this position, known as *due*; Coptic and Muslim traditions, too, use it in their religious observances. Representing salutation and an expression of awe, this is body-language at its most archaic. (*Ras al-Khaimah Museum*)

RIGHT: Senior guardian of the excavations at Hili. The guardian of the Hili tombs will use the gesture described opposite in his prayers five times a day. The similarity between the two wise, bearded faces is purely incidental, but the contemporary use by millions of this gesture, depicted 2000 years ago on the bone carving opposite and known for at least twice that long, is not.

A burial dating back to the second half of the second millennium BC, oriented in an east–west direction excavated at the pre-Iron Age and Iron Age site of al-Qusais. These two skeletons are the remains of a woman and a man, buried in an unusual and both literally and emotionally touching position, with their arms and legs intertwined, clearly indicating their relationship. (*Dubai Museum*)

LEFT: One can spend a long time among the dunes without seeing a living thing, but the sands always reveal traces of the hundreds of creatures which have crossed them. These range from the almost invisible spoors of tiny insects, to the large imprints of desert foxes, gazelles and camels, not to mention four-wheel drives. Here, two lizards approached each other, their paths crossed, leaving behind them the traces of a hectic sort of dance, and, probably seconds later, they turned towards the crest of the dune, continuing on their separate ways.

25

LEFT: A six-year-old school girl attending one of her frequent art classes in an Abu Dhabi school. The art-work created by five- to eight-year-olds in the schools of the Emirates is astonishing. In the past, with the exception of older boys who would encounter calligraphy when they learned to write, the children of this region rarely had a formal occasion to develop their visual aesthetic sense.

TOP: A collage made by a six-year-old from the same school.

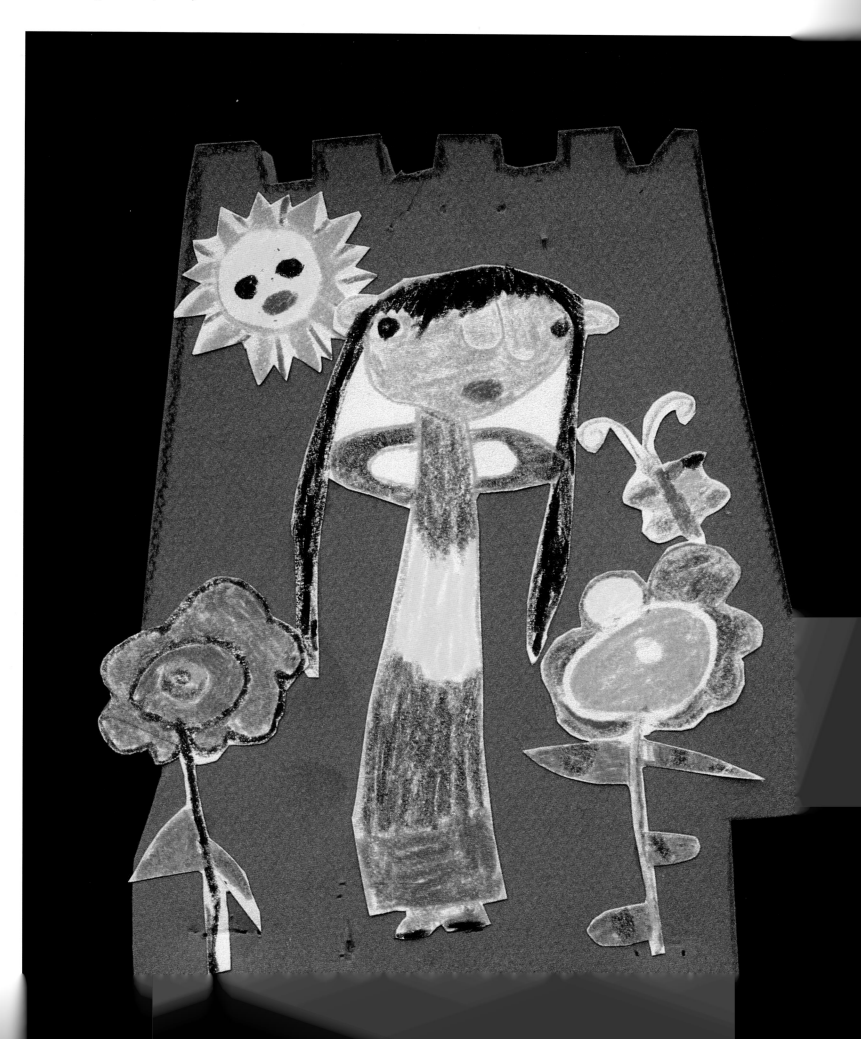

An island in Umm al-Qaiwain, home to a massive colony of Socotra cormorants, one of nearly one hundred species of bird known to breed in the Emirates. It would be impossible actually to count the myriad life-forms renewing themselves in the coastal waters of the Gulf, but this great concentration of large birds is a clear indication of the unlimited supply of available food.

The headquarters of Dubai's Chamber of Industry and Commerce, Dubai. One of the very latest high-rise towers of the Emirates, this building is designed to take the crucially important and contemporary role of Dubai's Chamber of Industry and Commerce through to the next millenium. From the outside, its peculiar design creates the visual illusion of a giant, weightless, translucent sheet, a bodiless shape suspended mid-flight between city and night sky.

The desert on the edge of the *Rub 'al-Khali* — the Empty Quarter. To experience the desert at night has left me sand-struck! It is not easy to describe the feeling of walking barefoot up the dunes and surfing down again under a full moon. I do not think it is an experience that can be communicated in words, and must hope that the image contains a resonance of what probably has to be experienced to be understood.

Dearer than castle and turret high
A tent and sound and breezes' sigh

(MAISOUM BINT BAHDAL)

The Bedouin tent, which was until recently an integral part of nomadic life and a typical sight from western Africa to the southern tip of Arabia, has vanished from the UAE. Even early travellers noticed the similarity of the tent's outline to that of its sand-dune surroundings. No other man-made dwelling blends more perfectly with its environment.

Ruins of al-Hiili fort, al-'Ain. This fortified mansion, abandoned by its owners for some time, has been in their possession for many generations. Their firm belief, based on coins found within the fort, is that it is at least five hundred years old.

MAIN PICTURE: A sudden but controlled escape of liquid gas burns off as a huge fireball. For a fraction of a second its shape is that of the firebird as it appears in ancient miniatures.

THE PHOENIX

The myth of the *'Anqa'* or Phoenix is the myth of the firebird, and as such, it is uniquely Arab. There are other legendary birds often called phoenixes – the Iranian *Simurgh*, the *Garuda* of Hindu myth and the Chinese *Feng-Huang* – but as attractive as they are, they lack the *'Anqa*'s deep roots in parable. The Ancient Greeks knew the myths of the *'Anqa'* and left us the earliest written evidence of their origin, pointing to the deserts of Arabia. There, myth said, in a desolate, barren chasm, the *'Anqa'* came into being, created by flames. This firebird is a huge, powerful and superbly beautiful creature, its fiery red plumage glowing at dusk and illuminating it from within. It is a symbol of incorruptible perfection. After a period of about five to six hundred years, the *'Anqa'* is supposed to return to its place of origin, and destroy itself by bursting into flames. Out of the pyre a new firebird – a new era – is born.

Like most legends, this one is not just a pretty tale. It contains elements of oral history, changed and embellished over thousands of years, but hinting at a memory and parabolic truth which our time is partly able to verify.

At least some fifteen thousand years ago, parts of Arabia were subjected to torrential rains, which carved the highest mountains of Arabia into the uniquely bizarre shapes they have today. Following centuries, possibly millennia, of floods, Arabia was for an extended period an enormously fertile region, carpeted with lush green vegetation. Periods of desiccation were followed by periods of sufficient rainfall to sustain widespread agriculture and an abundance of game. Even as late as the thirteenth century AD, Arabia was not yet the desiccated 'Empty Quarter' which to a great extent it is today. While this constitutes evidence of a cyclical rebirth, other evidence, given by place names and geological discoveries indicates that fire was found within today's Emirates in the most unlikely places.

The first successful oil well stands on the offshore island of Umm an-Nar, Mother of Fire. This name could be anything from two hundred to five thousand years old, but it is clear that it predates the discovery of oil in the gulf. What is more, there is some archeological evidence to suggest that a community lived and traded extensively from this Island as long as five thousand years ago. Could this community have witnessed the the desert catching fire? Half a century ago, a prominent archeologist and explorer named Harry St John Bridger Philby – better known now for the notoriety of his son, probably the most famous spy in British history – tried, without success, to find the legendary Atlantis of Arabia. He gave up when, after many difficult and risky attempts, he realized that the strange place within the Empty Quarter – Umm al-Hadid, Mother of Iron – that he had been exploring was not the foundation of an ancient megapolis, but the huge double-crater of an extinct volcano. While for Philby this represented the disappointment of a lifetime of exploration and digging, for those interested in verifying the basis of the myth of the firebird, it is an absorbing discovery; the ancient legend of the fiery phoenix still holds good as a fundamentally truthful parable of change.

PAST, PRESENT AND FUTURE I

This Neolithic stone scraper – one of the oldest artifacts found in the Emirates – comes from Habshan, in the Western Region of Abu Dhabi. Neolithic peoples wandered this region about seven thousand years ago, when it was less arid and more abundantly supplied with wildlife than it is today. (*al-'Ain museum*)

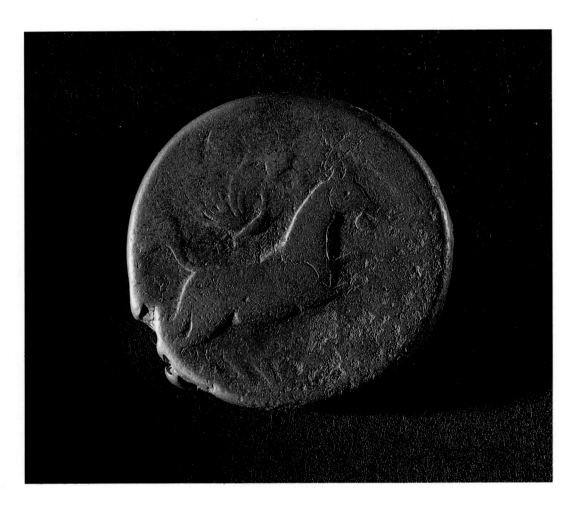

Bronze coin emblazoned with a horse emblem, minted between AD 1699 and 1757. One of 381 bronze coins discovered inside a jar in a farm at Mirbah. (*Fujairah Museum*)

RIGHT: Ostrich egg vessel, *c.* 2000 BC. This ostrich egg may have had a ritual rather than a domestic purpose. It was found buried with pottery and other objects at Qidfa tomb 1, Fujairah. The ostrich only became extinct in Arabia early this century. (*Fujairah Museum*)

Painted jar from Hili. This small, globular jar, dating from *c.* 2200 BC, was discovered in a collective tomb at Hili North. (*al-'Ain Museum*)

RIGHT: The northwest entrance of Hili tomb. Dating from *c.* 2500 BC, this pillbox shaped structure of carefully dressed stones at Hili, near al-'Ain, was a collective grave. The entrance, oriented towards the sunrise, is decorated with relief carvings of an embracing couple, an equestrian, a warrior with a club, and two leopards tearing at a smaller animal.

FOLLOWING PAGE: The southeast entrance of Hili tomb. The tableau above this doorway portrays a human couple hand in hand, confronting a pair of finely drawn oryx.

Pottery vessel of fine red ware, from Umm an-Nar. Sited near the present-day Abu Dhabi bridge. Umm an-Nar island was a substantial settlement and a centre of long-distance commerce in the third millennium BC. This vessel is thought to date from between 2700 and 2300 BC. (*al-'Ain Museum*)

RIGHT: This grey pottery vessel was among the grave goods discovered in the Hili tombs, and dates from between 2500 and 2000 BC. It is decorated with panels containing animal designs. (*al-'Ain Museum*)

Incised stone vessel from al-'Ain. Found at Qattarah — one of the original villages of the oasis — this gracefully tapering vessel is fluted and stands on a decorated base. It dates from the second millennium BC, when Qattarah was an important centre of bronze production, exporting fine swords and daggers, and importing tin. (*al-'Ain Museum*)

TOP: Chlorite beaker from al-'Ain. Combining a tapering neck with a bulbous base, and decorated with pierced, concentric circles, this vessel was found in the Hili tomb. It dates from *c.*2200 BC. (*al-'Ain Museum*)

RIGHT: A beautifully designed pendant in animal form, is cast in electrum — an alloy of gold and silver. It was discovered in a collective tomb at Qattarah, al-'Ain, and dates from *c.*1800 BC. (*al-'Ain Museum*)

FOLLOWING PAGE: Reconstructed beehive tombs near al-'Ain. The ancient peoples of the area interred their dead in burial chambers like these, hundreds of which have been discovered at the eastern foot of Jebel Hafit, near al-'Ain. Dating from before 3000 BC, the tombs have been found to contain imported pottery and locally made copper items, which comprised the grave goods of the dead.

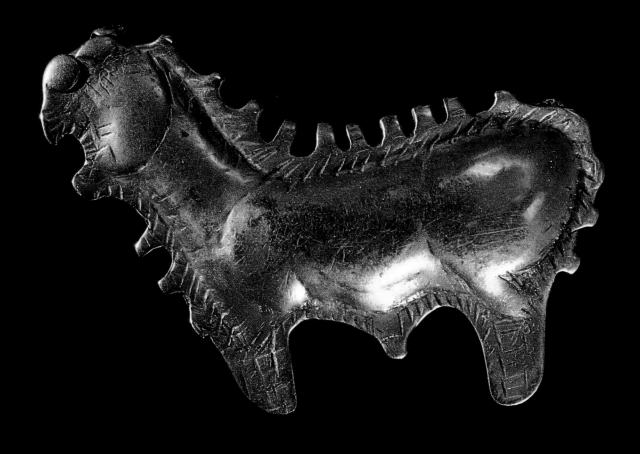

The pre-Iron Age and Iron Age site of al-Qusais, between 2000 and 1000 BC, is believed to be the largest settlement of that period in the Gulf region. More than one hundred and twenty graves between 40 and 180 centimetres have been excavated. Grave goods comprise pottery, stone and bronze objects, weapons including daggers, sticks, arrowheads and implements made of shells, and seashells filled with kohl for cosmetic use.

TOP AND BOTTOM: Many jars and other vessels embellished with snake motifs, and small undulating bronze snakes have been recovered from the 'Mount of Serpents', most likely a place of worship at al-Qusais dating back to the first millennium BC. (*Dubai Museum*)

RIGHT: One of the al-Qusais burials dating to the first millennium BC. This north–south oriented oval-shaped grave contained a human skeleton in a crouched position holding in its raised hand a small cup. (*Dubai Museum*)

Early irrigation channels, near al-ʿAin. Men learned to control the precious rainwater running off the Hajar mountains as early as five thousand years ago, when they became farmers and stockbreeders on the plains. These channels date from around 1000 BC.

Silver coins of Greek and local style. Minted between 300 and 200 BC, these coins were discovered at the site of Ad-Dour, in Umm al-Qaiwain Emirate, and indicate a flourishing foreign trade during that period. (*al-'Ain Museum*)

RIGHT: Bronze axe from Hili, al-'Ain. Discovered in an extensive Iron Age site about two kilometres from the Hili tombs, this axe dates from a period when copper production was increasing in the region, due to improvements in the design of furnace and bellows. (*al-'Ain Museum*)

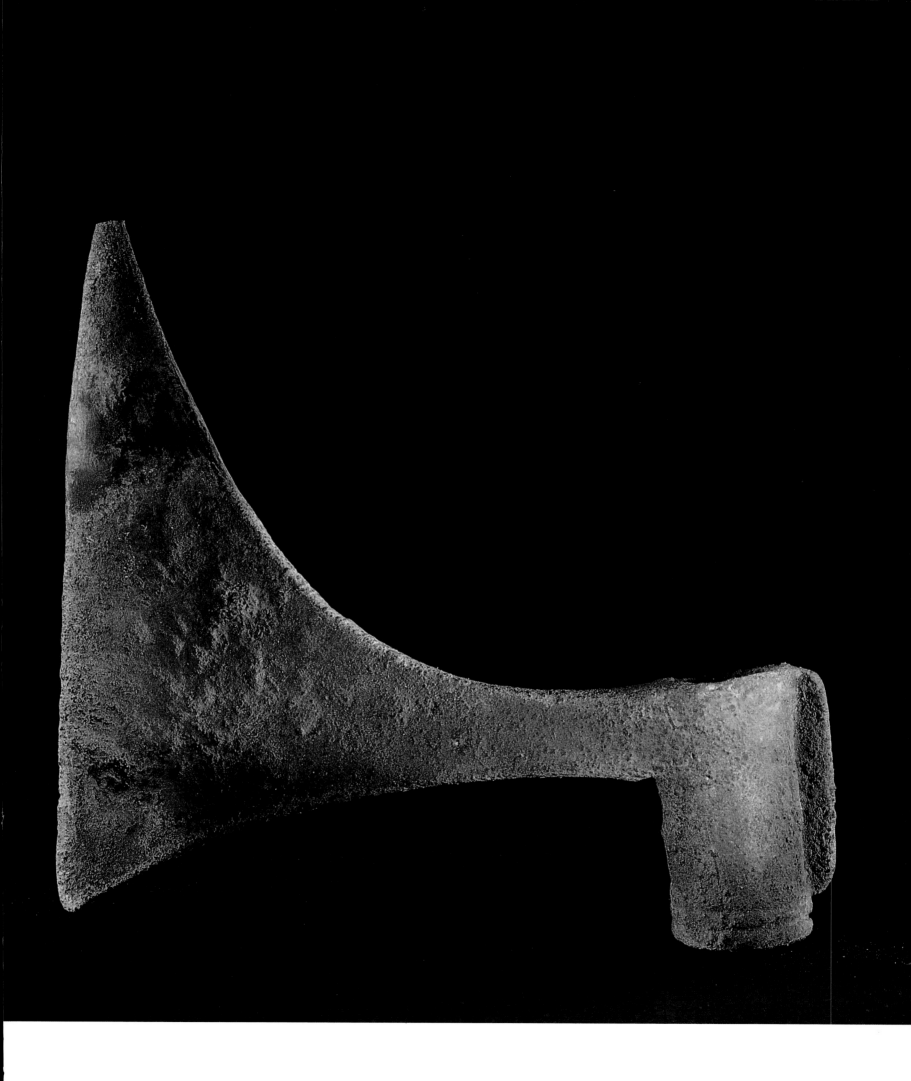

Rectangular chlorite vase. Found in a tomb at Fashgah in the Wadi al-Qawr, this vessel — undoubtedly a burial object — dates from the Iron Age, between 900 and 500 BC. In prehistoric times the region was famous for its production of chlorite or softstone, which was quarried locally. (*Ras al-Khaimah Museum*)

RIGHT: Pendant with carnelian bead necklace. Cast in electrum, the pendant shows the double-ended goat or horse motif typical of the period. Found in the cemetery at Dhaiyah, Ras al-Khaimah, the piece dates from the Bronze Age — about 2000 BC. (*Ras al-Khaimah Museum*)

FOLLOWING PAGE: Ruins of 'Refuge City', Ras al-Khaimah Emirate. Concealed and inaccessible, defended by the craggy foothills, this ancient settlement was a place of refuge until relatively recently. It remains unapproached by road or path.

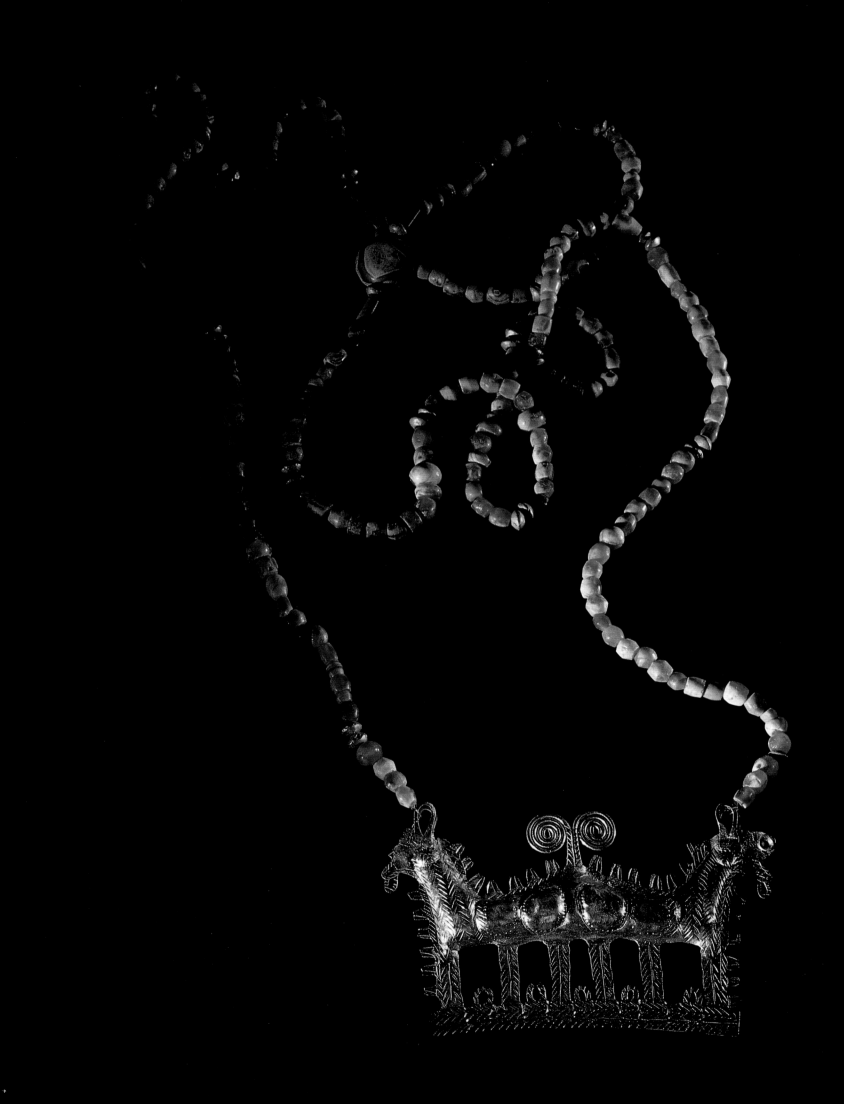

Irrigation channels at al-'Ain. The extensive palm groves and gardens at al-'Ain have depended for thousands of years on efficient artificial irrigation systems, the most important of which – the *aflaaj* – were subterranean conduits drawing liquid by the force of gravity from the local water table, and feeding it into the gardens via open channels.

RIGHT: Water bailiffs at al-'Ain oasis. The 'wise men' or *'urafaa'* traditionally regulated the flow of water from the *aflaaj*. Drawn from the most trusted families of the oasis, the bailiffs allotted a period of flow to each garden according to size, judging the time accurately from a sundial in daylight hours, and by the stars at night.

PRECEDING PAGE: Water terraces in the Hajar Mountains. In these rocky hills, with their sparse moisture from the winter rainfall, there exists in places almost no topsoil. Agriculture was only possible in a few of the valleys, where terraces such as these could be constructed to retain the vital soil.

ABOVE AND RIGHT: After their visit, the *'urafaa'* travel to the source of water, at some distance from al-'Ain, to inspect maintenance and reconstruction work on the subterranean ducts leading down to the oasis. Here they take coffee after a meal.

View from a watchtower, al-'Ain. Such towers — used as both lookouts and defensive bastions by the settled farmers — have been built in the Emirates since prehistoric times.

RIGHT: Fortified dwellings, al-'Ain. Throughout its history, the oasis was constantly under threat from foreign invaders or marauding Bedouin from the desert, and subject to clashes between its dominant tribes — the Dhawahir and the Na'im.

ABOVE AND LEFT: Sheer cliffs in the Hajar mountains. Cut out by tons of debris carried by the spates over eons, such *cuestas* – mild slopes ending in sudden, sheer drops – are a notable feature of these hills.

Hoard of historic coins. In the absence of a banking system, the settled peoples of the Emirates once hid or buried their savings in ceramic jars like this one. The coins here are about three hundred years old. (*al-'Ain Musuem*)

LEFT: The courtyard of al-Heeli fort, with its twenty-metre deep well upon which the dwelling is centred — a vitally important source of water in times of siege.

PRECEDING PAGE: Ruins of al-Heeli fort, al-'Ain. Inhabited up to two generations ago, this fortified dwelling stands among palm groves and gardens, a testimony to the raids, skirmishes and feuds to which the farmers were formerly subjected.

Ruins in the Hajar mountains, Fujairah Emirate. Such columns, constructed of stone and covered with alabaster, are typical of the architecture of the Fujairah region. The ruins shown are of a fortified palace in the Wadi Hail.

Sunset on the summit of Jebel Hafit.

Wadi on the western side of Jebel Hafit. Carved by raging spates of rainwater over the millennia, this is one of several wadis in which prehistoric tumuli have been discovered, dating back to about 3200 BC. The precarious rock formations in the background are further products of intense erosion by water.

BELOW: Western view from Jebel Hafit. Looking across the barren, highly eroded mountain surface, this view shows a good example of gentle slopes terminating in steep *cuestas*.

RIGHT: Geological formations, Jebel Hafit. Powerful erosive forces are at work on Jebel Hafit, where, owing to lack of soil or vegetation, rainwater runs off rapidly and begins to chisel at the surface of the rock. The peculiar rock stacks shown here appear to be close to collapse.

Sand dunes near al-'Ain. The dunes are formed by sand blown up the gentle windward slopes by the prevailing wind and sifting down the steeper leeward slopes. The knife-blade edges of the dune crests are composed of the finest sand grains, graded out by the wind. The sands appear to change colour from an hour before sunrise to an hour after sunrise.

LEFT: New road up Jebel Hafit. A vast fin of limestone, 1160 metres in height and oriented almost exactly north–south, Jebel Hafit dominates the landscape around al-'Ain oasis. The serpentine road seen here was recently constructed to conduct sight-seers to a viewpoint on its summit.

THE DESERT

Deserts are exploited for their mineral wealth and fossil deposits. Their recognition as a habitat of unparalleled grandeur lags far behind. Indigenous dignity and splendour is today traded for sand-slope skiing and noisy buggy dune-bashing, while amplified disco decibels invade millennia of silence. A few starry-eyed romantics believe such gaieties to be out of place, trivial, even somewhat vulgar. Their desert is one of giants shifting, on the move for 30,000 years, carrying with them a myriad of unseen life forms as ancient as themselves, a territory of absolute perfection of shapes and textures, of tactile sensuousness in timeless flux.

The desert was and is an unforgiving environment. It has its way with trespassers. Sobering mementoes are not rare. Decades ago, driving on a winter night toward Ulan Bator on the Mongolian plateau I came across a lorry driver turned icicle. Less than an hour earlier he had stopped, leaned against the warm engine cowling, lit a cigarette and dozed off. If death by freezing is not a hazard often associated with desert travel, dehydration is. Shortly after the Mongolian experience, stuck in the Sahara some hundred miles out of Khartoum, I got a foretaste of it; it is a taste that lingers for some time.

With the exception of the Nile's desert edge, I never chanced upon a snake in the desert, though their presence cannot be doubted. Arabian dunes are embellished with graceful lines, the sinuous footsteps of snakes. Desert protocol requires that a respectful distance is kept, especially from the carpet viper: rumour has it that those who neglect this necessary etiquette regret it for the rest of their lives – that is to say about eight seconds.

LEFT: Jebel Hafit – a view from the summit at sunset. This view shows the road cutting through the vast, flat alluvial plains which surround the mountain. The relative fertility of these plains is due to abundant run-off of rainwater from both Jebel Hafit and the adjacent mountains of Oman.

PRECEDING PAGE

Jebel Hafit at night. Until the 1960s, there was no electricity in the al-'Ain area. Today the brooding night is split asunder by streams of sodium lights running deep into the desert. The road up Jebel Hafit appears on the right.

FOLLOWING PAGES

The luxurious green growth at Hatta, one of the principal oases and surrounded by the highest sand dunes in the Emirates, is due to the subterranean irrigation system known as *aflaaj*.

MAIN PICTURE: It is a mistake to believe that there is just one kind of desert. Even in the limited territory of the Emirates there are quite different sorts, and we are still only speaking here of those made up of sand dunes. As we can see from this almost flamingo-pink image, far from being of an overall yellow-brown, the desert can display striking variations of colour. And sometimes the wind draws the sand into the sorts of whirlpool-dunes seen here, with sides that are perhaps a hundred feet high.

An inhabitant of al-'Ain oasis visiting the other principal oasis of the Abu Dhabi Emirate at Liwa. His face is well-protected against sand and sun.

PAST, PRESENT AND FUTURE II

Lizard tracks on rippled sand. The desert might seem a dead world during the day, but its appearance is deceptive. Due to its forbidding diurnal temperatures, most desert animals venture out by night, leaving only the pattern of their tracks to tell of their passing.

FOLLOWING PAGES

A camel train returning home at sunset in the desert east of al-'Ain after a day spent taking tourists into the desert.

The double-horned *rahl*, or 'North Arabian' camel saddle – introduced after about 500 BC – was a revolutionary design, allowing a mounted warrior to fight on camel-back for the first time. It remains in use in many parts of the Arab world today. (*al-'Ain Museum*)

PRECEDING PAGES

Sand dunes at Liwa on the edge of the *Rub 'al-Khali* — the Empty Quarter.

Crest of a dune in the *Rub 'al-Khali*.

Untended oasis. This small stand of grass and palm trees has flourished where the water table is near to the surface. While some of the date palms may once have been tended, the 'oasis' has now grown wild.

Hooded falcons at Liwa. A traditional sport with its origin in prehistoric hunting, hawking has remained popular in the Emirates. Carefully tended and hooded, these falcons at Liwa are frequently taken on desert forays by their Bedu owners, although their traditional prey, the Houbara bustard, and the Cape hare, are now protected.

PRECEDING PAGES: When they are not hunting, falcons like to rest and dose in semidarkness. Even when they are taken out into the desert light for exercise they are hooded and carried on camel-back, relaxed and half asleep. But once their hoods are removed they become agitated and liable to fly off.

LEFT: After a longish trip through the desert the bird feels hot under its hood and welcomes a cold shower!

TOP: Tribesmen enjoying conversation by the fireside. Because of their necessary mobility, the Bedouin remained poor in material culture, placing emphasis instead on the luxury of language and valuing rhetoric and oral poetry above all other arts. These Bedouin, though seen here with camels for purposes of the photograph, are today more likely to be found driving motorcars.

ABOVE: Bedouin meeting in the desert. Though an important and powerful group, the Bedouin probably never comprised more than 10 per cent of the entire population of the Emirates, their numbers decreasing during affluent periods. Here the tribesmen exchange the traditional embrace and nose-kiss reserved for close friends and members of the same tribe.

Bedouin with their camels. No longer the hardy animals which made the Bedouin way of life possible in the past, the camels of the Emirates have today become accustomed to eat processed feed and drink water daily. They are now treated more as pets than as work animals.

ABOVE: Camels outside al-'Ain. First domesticated in southern Arabia around 3000 BC, and for millennia the mainstay of the desert economy, the camel remains a favourite animal in the Emirates, though it is seldom ridden in earnest today except in races. The camels shown here, now used to give short rides to tourists, are carrying saddles of tubular steel, specially designed for the purpose.

LEFT: One of 381 bronze coins, minted between 1700 and 1760 AD discovered inside a jar in a farm at Mirbah. (*Fujairah Museum*)

ABOVE AND FOLLOWING PAGE: Livestock market, al-'Ain. Camels, once brought on the hoof to al-'Ain by Bedouin tribesmen from as far away as southern Oman, are today transported more easily in Toyota pick-ups. A few are sold for stud, milk or riding, but the great majority are destined for the butcher's block.

Traditional reed-built dwelling. Known locally as a *barasti*, such houses were the most common type of dwelling in the Emirates in pre-oil years. Constructed of dried reeds or palm fronds, they were valued for their coolness in the humid summers. Also on display are traditional mats, food covers and other objects braided from palm fibre.

RIGHT: Gateway to the old *souq*, al-'Ain. In days long past, this ruined archway of mud-brick formed the entrance to a bustling market. Inside, palm trees bloom where merchants' stalls once stood.

Sodom apple, *Calotropis procera*. Found almost everywhere except the most arid desert, the waxy-leafed Calotropis is browsed only by the unselective goat. Its grapefruit-sized fruit contains a poisonous white liquid capable of blinding a human being.

RIGHT: Colours and textures in the sand. The desert sands are a kaleidoscope of every conceivable colour, due to their different mineral constituents; their textures also vary due to the size of the grains and the continually shifting eddies of the wind.

FOLLOWING PAGES

Water in a wadi-bed near Hatta. In the hot summers the flow in wadis such as this one dwindles and threatens to dry up completely.

Dead palm sapling, Liwa. In the past, palm saplings were hand-irrigated by the local tribesmen until their roots reached the water table. Neglected by its owner, this young palm has expired before establishing contact with the aquifer.

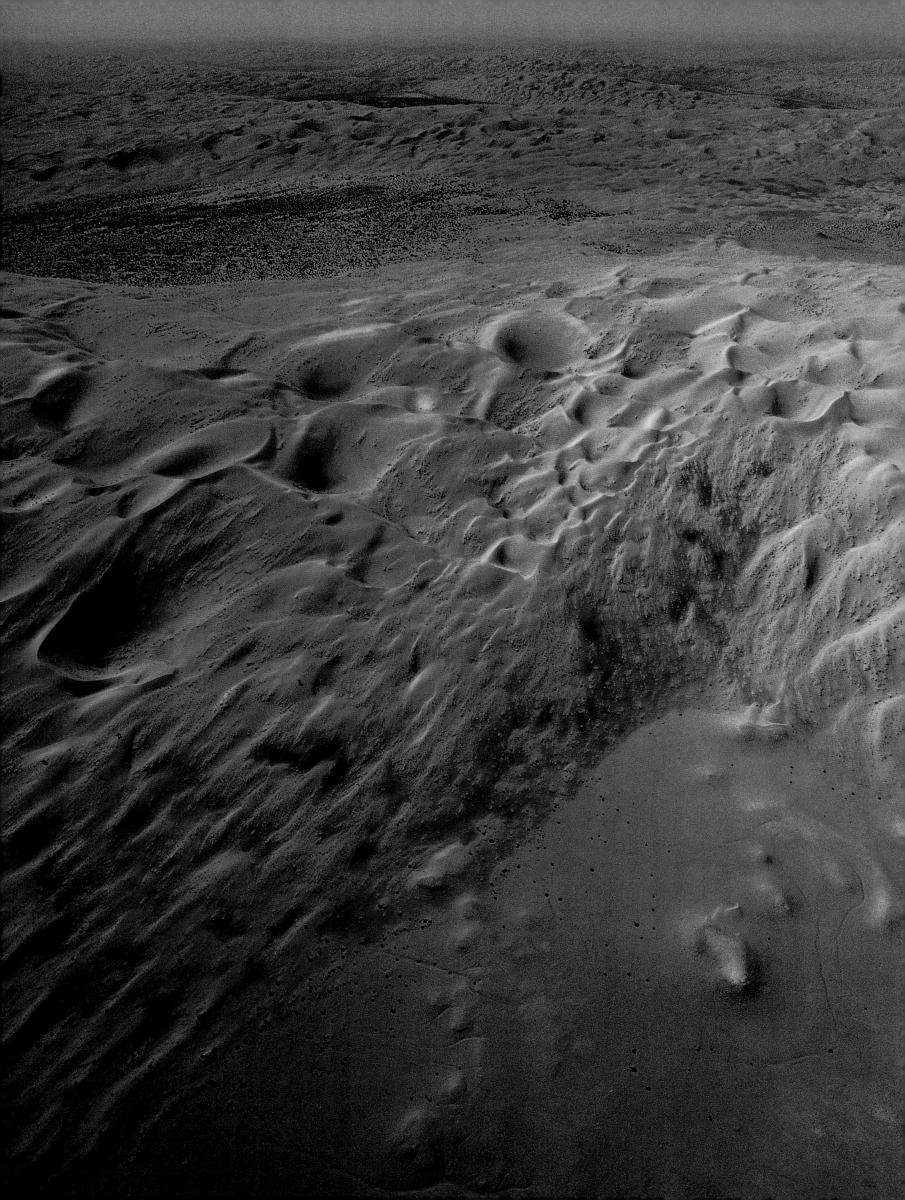

RIGHT: A date palm – 'the prince of trees' – al-'Ain. Until recently, dates were the major source of nourishment in this region of Arabia, since they were high in calories and could be kept indefinitely when dried. Always cut just before ripening, the preharvest dates display many colours from bright red to saffron yellow: thirty-six different varieties of date are known in the Emirates alone.

BELOW: Cabbages growing at Liwa. In past times little else but date trees could be cultivated at Liwa, because of the absence of any irrigation system and the infertility of the soil. Trees had to be watered individually from heavy waterbags carried by hand. Today, the mechanical pump has greatly increased the possibilities of cultivation.

Interior, Ras al-Khaimah fort, now a museum. The picture shows the careful renovation work which has been undertaken.

RIGHT: Wind-tower, Ras al-Khaimah fort. Probably originating among Persian immigrants in the nineteenth century, the wind-tower or *badgir* is a unique feature of the architecture of the Emirates. The structure acts as a scoop channelling the wind into the building – often directly into the sleeping-quarters – to cool the humid coastal nights.

The inner courtyard, Ras al-Khaimah fort, showing external stairways with recently-added wooden bannisters.

Carved door, Ras al-Khaimah fort. Found in both forts and private houses, such doors were mostly imported from India. They frequently held great sentimental value for their owners, who would take them along when moving house. Many bore a verse from the Quran on the lintel.

RIGHT: Detail of carved door, Ras al-Khaimah fort.

ABOVE AND RIGHT: Fortified dwellings, al-'Ain. Such fortresses
provided refuge for both men and and animals in time of attack.

PRECEDING PAGE: Main entrance, al-'Ain fort. One of the many forts
belonging to the al-Nahyan family – rulers of Abu Dhabi – who
acquired overlordship over the oasis in the mid nineteenth century.

Watchman at Bithna Fort, Fujairah Hills. In the past, tribesmen like this one had the task of scanning the horizons for raiders. Today, the old man – who has no surviving relatives – performs nominal duties as caretaker of the fort, in return for food and shelter in one of its towers.

RIGHT: Bithna Fort, Fujairah Emirate. In former times, the survival of local settlements depended on such fortresses, which are scattered throughout Fujairah and the rest of the Emirates.

BELOW: Date palms, Hatta oasis. Once a traditional village, now a favourite weekend spot for local tourists from Dubai, this luxuriant settlement in the Hajar mountains has been inhabited since at least 2000 BC.

RIGHT AND FOLLOWING PAGE: Irrigation channels and cisterns at Hatta. A small enclave of Dubai Emirate on the western side of the Hajar mountains, Hatta nestles against the border with Oman. The oasis is rich in gardens and palm groves watered by irrigation channels, fed from cisterns like these.

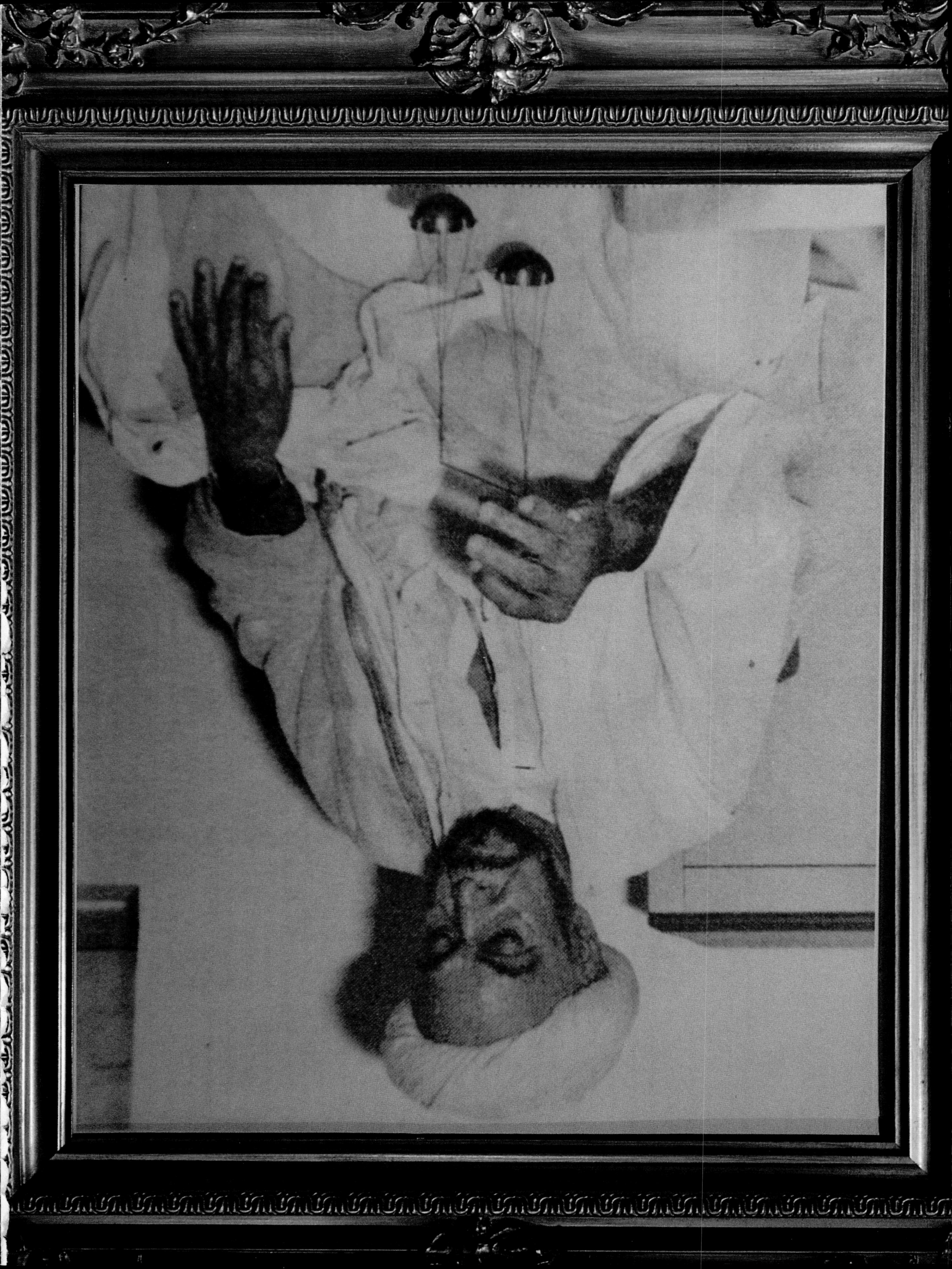

THE SEA

The cultures of the Gulf had few trade commodities on which they could depend. The most important ones of the past were dates, minerals, frankincense and pearls. The present economy of the Emirates is based, of course, on petroleum, which today overshadows these earlier, crucially important commodities.

There is no pearl fishing any more in the Gulf, and the reason why the Gulf's oysters no longer grow pearls has not been established. The trade in pearls still exists, but the flow of pearls now moves in the opposite direction to that which it took in the nineteenth century when it was the principal source of income for the area. Today the pearl is appreciated in the Emirates both for its beauty and as a symbol of bygone ways of life. For centuries the most beautiful and perfect pearls invariably ended up at the courts of India and Europe. These same pearls are now brought back to the Emirates by its own people who often treasure them simply for the pleasure of appreciating their beauty in private, not bothering to string or incorporate them in other pieces of jewellery for public display. Some of today's collectors have amassed enormous numbers of pearls of all sizes, hues and quality which they bring out of the strongroom in large sacks to savour from time to time. Then, reluctantly, they put them back in the sacks, sealing them carefully and returning them to the strongroom.

LEFT: A storage jar made of pottery found at the ruins of ancient Julfar in Ras al-Khaimah (c. fifteenth century AD). This jar has three handles and may have been used for storing dates or cereals. The red circles, placed without any evident symmetry, give it a unique and timeless appearance. (al-'Ain Museum)

FOLLOWING PAGE: A dhow leaving Dubai Creek in the early morning. These vessels, built entirely of wood, still connect the Gulf coast with far-flung ports. Today the average trip to Indian ports takes nine to twelve days, but in earlier times, if the winds were contrary, the voyage might have taken a good deal longer. Similar vessels sailing the same routes over the centuries invariably carried a cargo of pearls.

MAIN PICTURE

LEFT: In the head office of the al-Fardan jeweller's empire hangs an historic photograph of Haji Ibrahim Hassan al-Fardan aged 110. He lived and worked as the outstanding expert of pearls, to the age of 115. The al-Fardan family has fished and traded in pearls for at least three generations, probably more.

CENTRE: Being spherical and luminously reflective, pearls lying en masse in this way bounce their light off one another giving an effect that you would never witness from pearls strung around a woman's neck. For the photographer this is an irresistible but troublingly difficult quality. It is an erie feeling to look down upon such a quantity of beautiful pearls.

RIGHT: Jawad al-Moosawi, general manager of al-Fardan jewellers, weighing pearls on the scale used by Haji Ibrahim Hassan al-Fardan in the first picture.

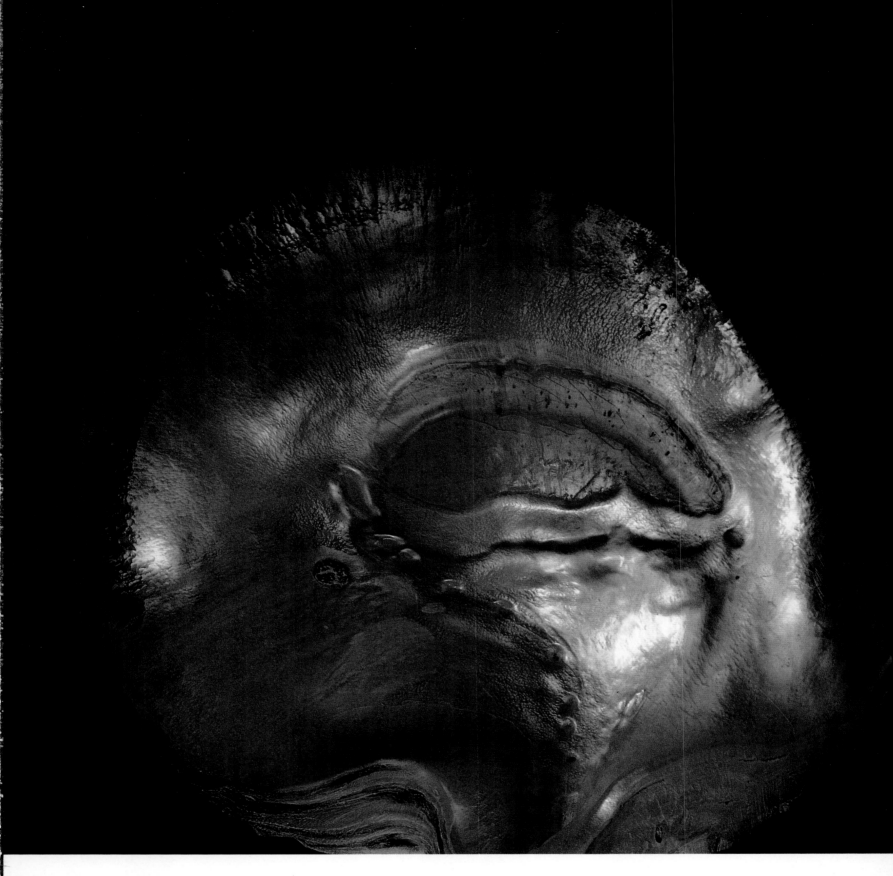

Inside of a pearl oyster. Generally the shell (or 'fish' as it is called) was discarded, but occasionally a particuarly beautiful example would be kept. The seeds in this one indicate that when first opened it would have confronted the onlooker with seven pearls. The nacre in this example is especially lustrous, evocative of the dreams of those who hoped to make their fortunes by finding a pearl of unimagineable size and beauty.

PAST, PRESENT AND FUTURE III

Ornate dhow helm. (*al-ʿAin Museum*)

Shipwrights building a model dhow. Such a model was traditionally launched prior to a ship's departure. If it survived a stormy sea, this was taken as a good omen for the voyage ahead. If it were dashed against the rocks, then it was believed that the sea had taken it in lieu of the mother ship. Whatever happened, therefore, the fate of the model provided a kind of spiritual insurance for the crew undertaking a long voyage.

RIGHT: First steps in construction of a dhow, Ajman wharf. Until Portuguese caravels appeared in the Gulf in the sixteenth century, dhow timbers were sewn together with coconut fibre rather than nailed, sails were rigged 'fore and aft' rather than square-rigged, and hulls were double-ended. The square stern shown in this picture is a direct descendant of Portuguese design.

FOLLOWING PAGE: The hull of a dhow under construction. By 300 BC Greeks commented on superior boat-building, especially the wood used, which were almost sea-water proof meaning that a boat could be in the sea for long period without suffering damage. Today the 'boom' or keel is always made of teak as is usually the rest of the dhow. Other woods used are mangrove (mainly for poles), jungle wood (for ribs). There is always a long wait to get these woods from India, meaning that construction takes a long time – about ten to twelve months for a large boat. The empty hull and deck will cost more than two million dirham, with the engine and other fittings adding a further milion dirham.

Dhow crewmen resting before a voyage. Asian and Arab seamen have been crossing the Indian Ocean by ship ever since prehistoric times, when they discovered the secret of the monsoon winds. Indian-crewed dhows like this one still carry on the trade with Bombay and the Malabar Coast – nine to eleven days out of Dubai.

RIGHT: Coastal village, between Ajman and Sharjah, believed to have been a pearl-fishers' colony. The building in the foreground is probably a mosque, while in the background stands a well-preserved watchtower whose function would have been to protect the village.

PRECEDING PAGE: The stern of a carefully refurbished dhow, now a pleasure boat, on Dubai Creek. Dhow owners are tempted to sell their vessels or convert them themselves from sea-going cargo vessels into luxurious crusiers. The wood-built dhow is still an expensive craft built from Lebanese cedar or from timber which even today is imported from as far away as the Cochin coast in India.

TOP, ABOVE AND RIGHT: 'Burning' or cauterizing with hot irons. A healer versed in traditional medicine demonstrates this ancient Arab panacea for ills ranging from broken limbs to mental disorders, using instruments from al-'Ain museum. The fine metal rods are held over an open flame until they are red-hot, and are then applied to the patient's skin – either directly to the affected region, or to key points such as the knuckles or behind the ears. The process has similarities with acupuncture.

Chinese dish, Sung-Yuan period. This dish in green celadon dates from the late Sung-early Yuan dynasties, and suggests trade connections between the Emirates and China as early as the fourteenth century AD. (*Ras al-Khaimah Museum*)

RIGHT: Chinese dish, Ming dynasty. This fine example of blue and white-patterned porcelain, dating from the Ming period – early seventeenth century – is convincing proof of the trading connections which traditionally linked the Emirates with the Far East. (*Ras al-Khaimah Museum*)

TOP: Pearls in graded sorting sieves. Part of the standard equipment of the pearl-traders, these sieves were used to grade the pearls into five different sizes, which were then sold in bulk. Only the largest pearls – over two grams in weight – would be sold individually.

ABOVE: Traditional pearl-weighing scales. These hand-held scales, also part of the merchant's kit, were used to determine the weight of pearls exceeding two grams. Though superseded by electronic digital scales of meticulous accuracy, the traditional instrument is still often preferred.

The world's largest pearl collection, Dubai. The descendant of one of Dubai's prominent families of pearl-merchants, Sultan Alowais acquired his own fortune from pearls then went into international banking in the post-oil age. He keeps this priceless collection of pearls out of personal interest and nostalgia for the past. A poet himself, Sultan has established the al-Owais Cultural Foundation which administers an annual prize for the best in Arab poetry, writing, science and culture.

Miscellaneous collection of pearls.

RIGHT: Pearl necklace with three strands. The pearling boom of the nineteenth century depended mainly on the popularity in the West of pearl necklaces, which were not only a sign of wealth, but also a symbol of the exotic Orient.

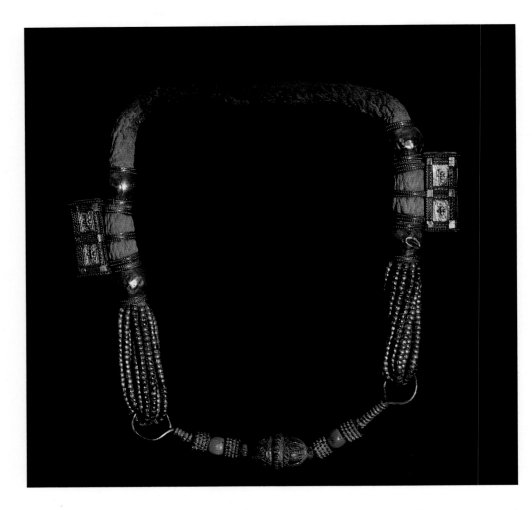

Historic ladies' jewellery. Such silver jewellery was traditionally the personal property of its owner, providing a sign of her marital status as well as a highly mobile asset that could be liquidated in times of need.

RIGHT: A woman wearing an elaborate silver headdress. (*al-'Ain Museum*)

The silver-smiths of Dubai, Sharjah and Ras al-Khaimah, who manufactured jewellery of the kind shown here and on the preceding page, often obtained the silver by melting down Maria Theresa silver dollars, which were still legal tender in the 1940s. (*al-'Ain Museum*)

LEFT: Traditional costume and jewellery. Such finery was traditionally reserved for weddings and other special occasions, and often represented the bride's share of the money paid to her family by the groom. (*al-'Ain Museum*)

BELOW: Painting designs with henna. Traditionally, this orange-brown dye was used to decorate the hands and feet at weddings and circumcisions, mainly among the townspeople. When completed, the designs are covered and left to dry. When dry, the crusted black paste is removed to reveal a delicate orange-brown pattern of dyed skin. The designs shown here reveal a contemporary Indian influence, while traditional designs were simple and geometric.

RIGHT: The elaborate henna-dying of hands and feet would have called for equally elaborate jewellery, including a tiara-like silver headdress, as here.

Entrance to a *madrasah*, Dubai. These higher Quranic
schools were rare in the Emirates in pre-oil times.

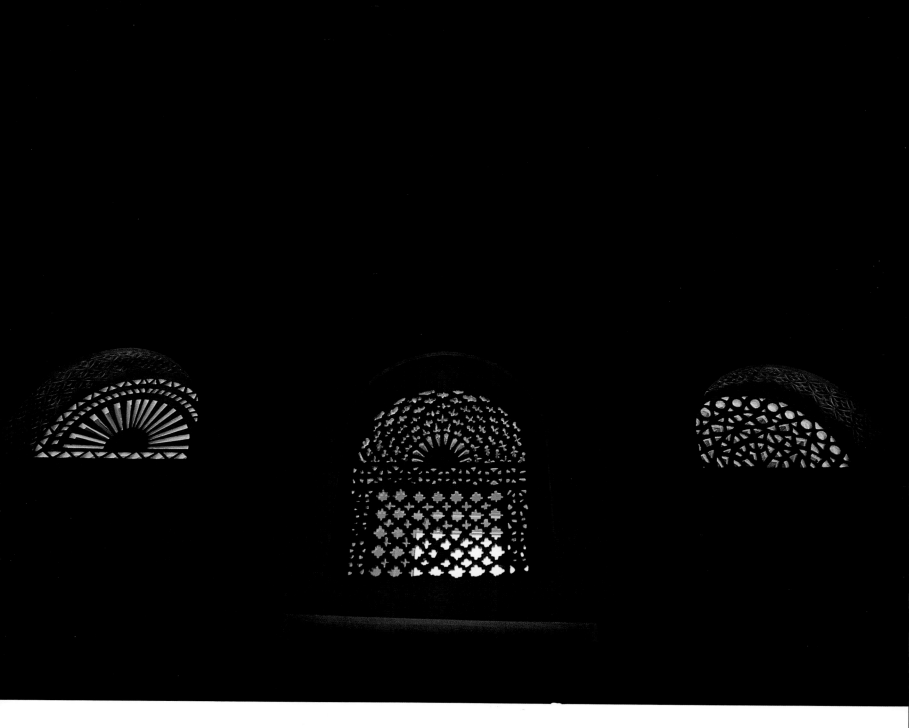

Ornate windows of a *madrasah*, Dubai.

LEFT: Detail from a medical manuscript by an unknown author. Written in Moroccan calligraphy, this page also shows a scalpel used in phlebotomy—the opening of veins. (*Juma Al Majid Center, Dubai*)

BELOW: Folio from an astronomical manuscript. Now one of the largest libraries in the Emirates, the Center was formed around a private collection of manuscripts assembled in pre-oil days by Juma al-Majid, a one-time pearl merchant who later became one of the world's wealthiest businessmen. These pages, from an eighteenth-century manuscript, show the relative positions of the sun, the moon, Jupiter and Venus. (*Juma Al Majid Center, Dubai*)

RIGHT: Folio from an astronomical text. A nineteenth-century transcription of a work by Ibn Sina (Avicenna), who died in 1047, the manuscript is entitled *Mukhtasar al-Majasti*, and belongs to the Juma Al Majid Center. This folio shows geometrical representations of astronomical motion. (*Juma Al Majid Center, Dubai*)

فيكون البعد الاول الذي بركو وهو ككا اصغر
من الوسط وإما اشكال الحال الثالثة وهي
هذه اخرج فيها برله توح بواوج
ابوجه الحال وذلك معلوم دقا عمل بعد
داوبه ح زح ما عمل فيل محربه ان المربح ديم
روي المشتري سياء او دبيقيا كو زحل
عشة دفايق من احذ بين ان السبع
والزوايا اذا كانت على ما اضنت زد

Traditional windows, Dubai. Designed to keep the light out rather than to let it in, these windows are cut in an ornate floral design with chinks to let cool air flow inside.

OPPOSITE: Round wind-tower Sharjah. The *badgir* or wind-tower was traditionally square, presenting one face to each direction of the wind. This unusual wind- tower, however, is cylindrical in shape with a capping dome and fine ornamental ceramic and plaster work.

FOLLOWING PAGE: Facade, Palace of Sheikh Sa'id, Dubai.

Interior court of Fujairah castle, seat of the Sharqiyyin rulers of Fujairah Emirate until well within living memory. In 1925 it was bombarded for ninety minutes by a British naval squadron, which caused extensive damage to three of its towers.

LEFT: Tower, Fujairah castle. Built of massive mud-brick walls strengthened by stones, this tower was also damaged in the bombardment of 1925.

PRECEDING PAGE: Fujairah castle, with ruins of old Fujairah town. The fortress was surrounded by houses which were inhabited until recently. Now in ruins, they are to be reconstructed to form a Heritage Site.

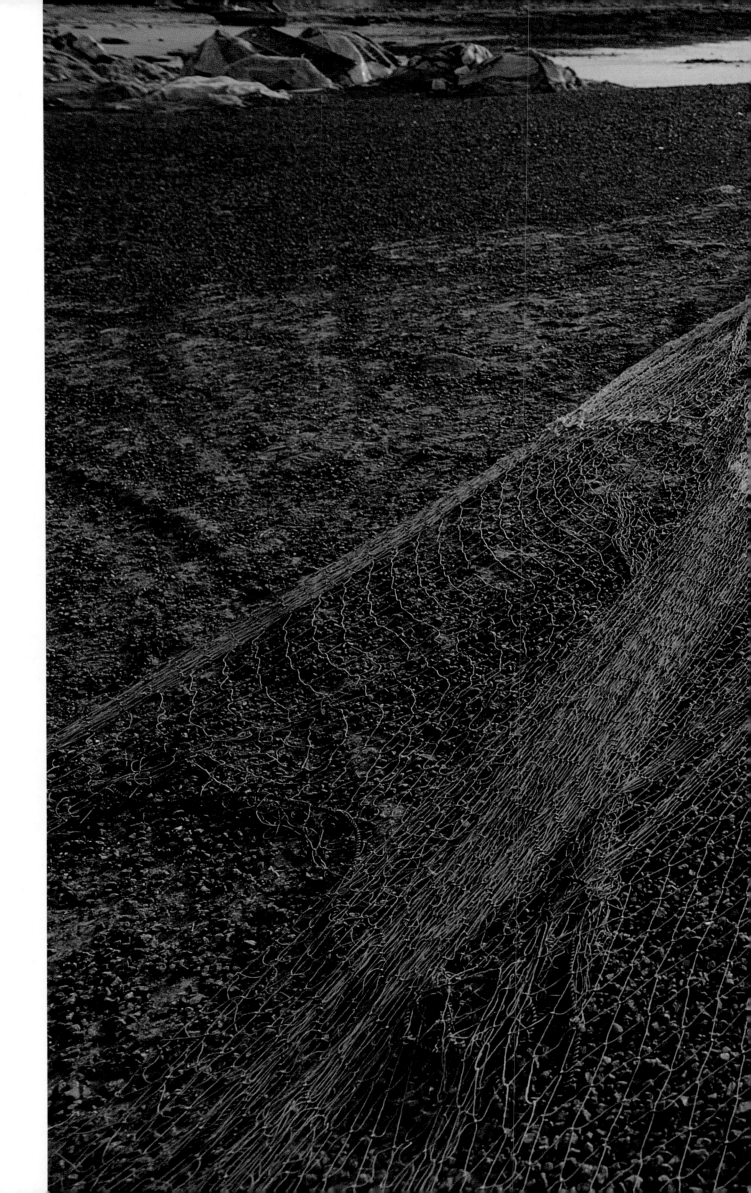

Fishermen drying sardines on the beach at Fujairah city. In the past, the Bedouin often depended on dried fish as summer-feed for their camels and goats, and cultivators needed it as fertilizer for their palm trees. Though less vital than previously, dried fish is still exported from the Emirates.

RIGHT: Island off the Fujairah coastline. One of the many hundreds of beautiful, deserted islands, both in the Gulf, and the Gulf of Oman, belonging to the United Arab Emirates.

PRECEDING PAGE: Fisherman repairing nets, Fujairah Emirate. Fishing has been a major part of Fujairah's economy since the earliest times. With access to the Gulf of Oman — reckoned to be one of the world's last great virgin fishing grounds — the Emirate has plans to expand its fishing industry in the near future.

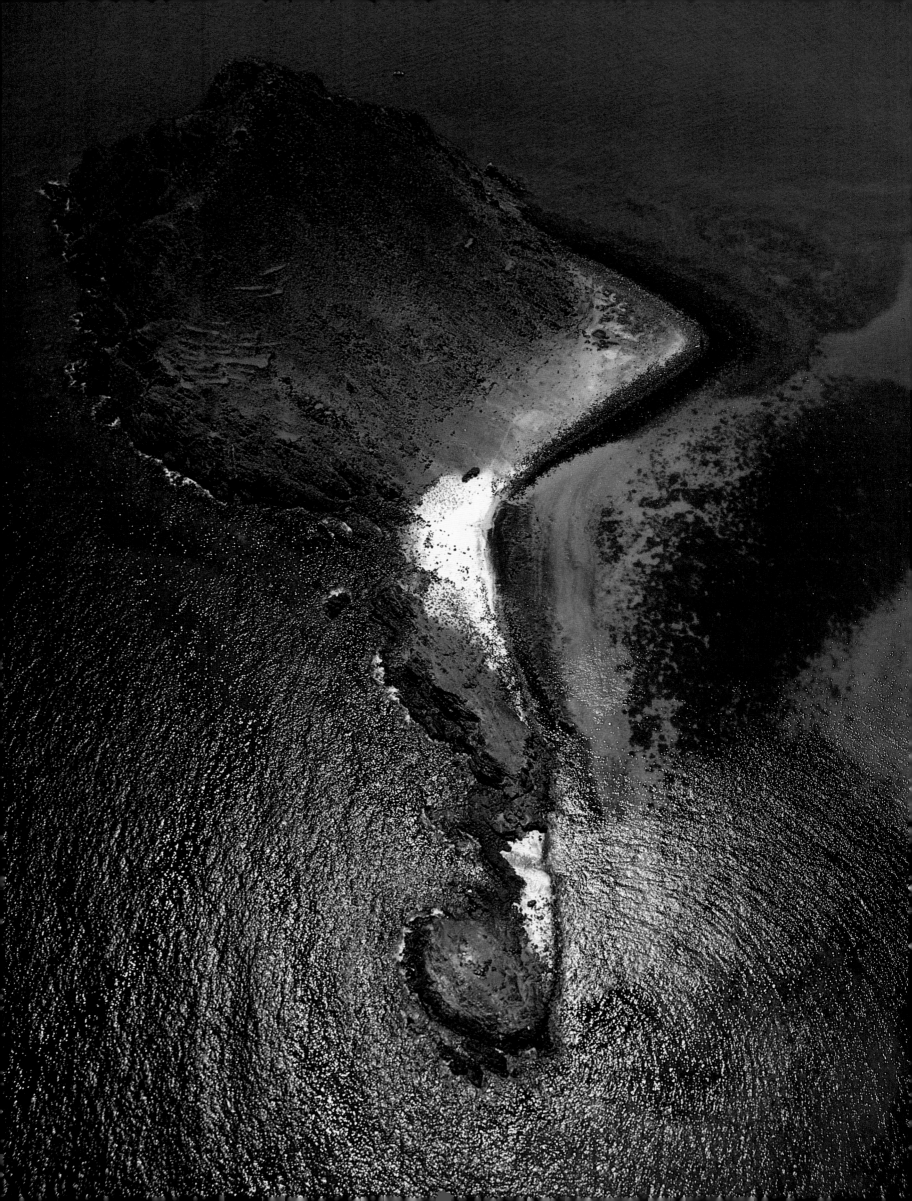

Baddiyah Mosque, Fujairah, believed to be the oldest mosque still in use in the UAE.

LEFT: A watchtower doorway at Baddiyah, Fujairah Emirate.

PRECEDING PAGE: Fujairah coastline, looking south. As the only one of the seven Emirates sited on the Gulf of Oman, Fujairah lies beyond the dangerous defile of the Straits of Hormuz and close to the major shipping routes across the Indian Ocean.

PRECEDING PAGE AND ABOVE: With its single central pillar, this building is the oldest Islamic structure in the Emirates. Lacking a minaret, and hidden at the base of a rocky hill, it may have been used for worship before Islam was fully accepted here. Local lore has it that the mosque of al-Baddiyah was endowed by a fisherman grateful for being led by Allah to find an unusually perfect and precious pearl. Nearby is the hamlet of Lu'lu'bia, which means 'the pearly place'. Whether the story of the fisherman is true is questionable; what is not in doubt is that the mosque is a pearl of Islamic architecture.

Traditional writing implements. Due to the scarcity of wood and paper, pupils in traditional Quranic schools (*Kuttaab*) wrote on the polished shoulder-blades of cows like this one, from which the writing could easily be erased with a damp cloth. Other scholastic accessories shown here are a glass inkwell, pens made of reeds, and an oil lamp, essential for lighting the dark school room, all of which were in use until the 1950s. (*al-'Ain museum*)

THE CITIES

The coastline of the Emirates has, with few exceptions, been sparsely populated, the reason for this being that most water sources produced brackish, undrinkable water, heavily contaminated by salty sea water. The few drinkable, sweet-water wells there were did not generally sustain a large concentration of people. The discovery of a potent source of excellent drinking water on the island of Abu Dhabi seems to have been accidental.

According to legend, about two hundred years ago a sheikh ruling the oasis of Liwa, some sixty miles inland, ordered a hunting party to travel across the desert towards the coast and to bring back some game. After days in the desert, the hunters spotted the recently made tracks of a gazelle, and followed the trail. The hunting party was unwittingly led across a narrow natural causeway to a large island. No sooner did they arrive on the island than they realized that they were cut off from the mainland by the incoming tide. Their water supply had run out, they were thirsty, and experience told them that they were unlikely to find any respite on the island.

Searching desperately for water they came upon the hoof prints of the gazelle once more, which led them straight to a spring of unusually palatable drinking water. Joyfully they filled their waterskins and, as soon as the outgoing tide allowed, they crossed over to the mainland and travelled back to the oasis of Liwa, bringing with them a far greater prize from their hunting expedition than meat. In recognition of the service it had done them, they called the island Abu Dhabi, the place of the Gazelle, after the elusive creature that led them there.

PAST, PRESENT AND FUTURE IV

One of the many brightly coloured municipal flower displays that are maintained all the year round between every streetlight in Abu Dhabi today – a city where flowers were previously unkown.

FOLLOWING PAGES

Close-up of telecommunications sphere atop the Etisalat building.

The old fort, Abu Dhabi. Once the home of the al-Bu Falah – later the al-Nahyan – Abu Dhabi's ruling family, the fort has been restored and now houses the Centre for Documentation and Research.

Bainunah Tower of the Hilton Hotel, Abu Dhabi.

Forte Grande Hotel, Abu Dhabi.

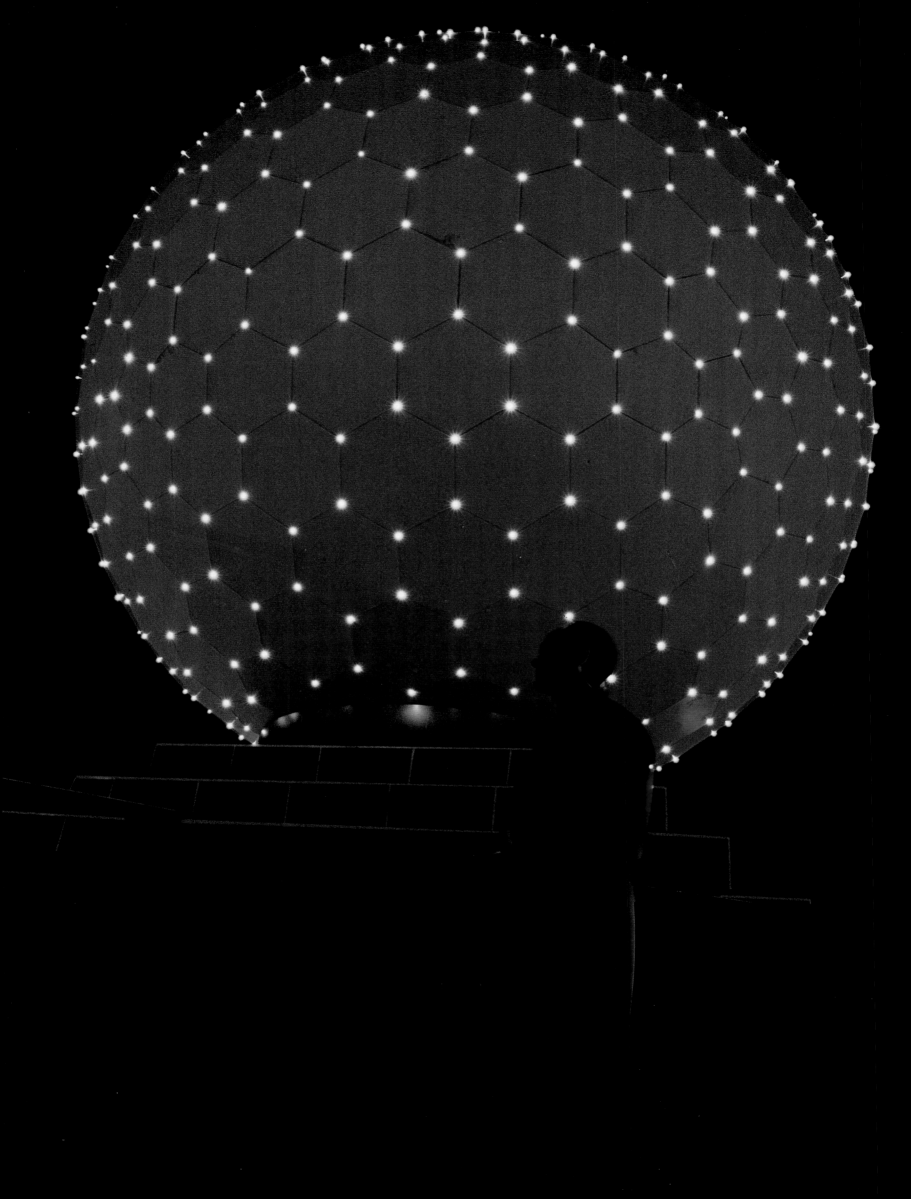

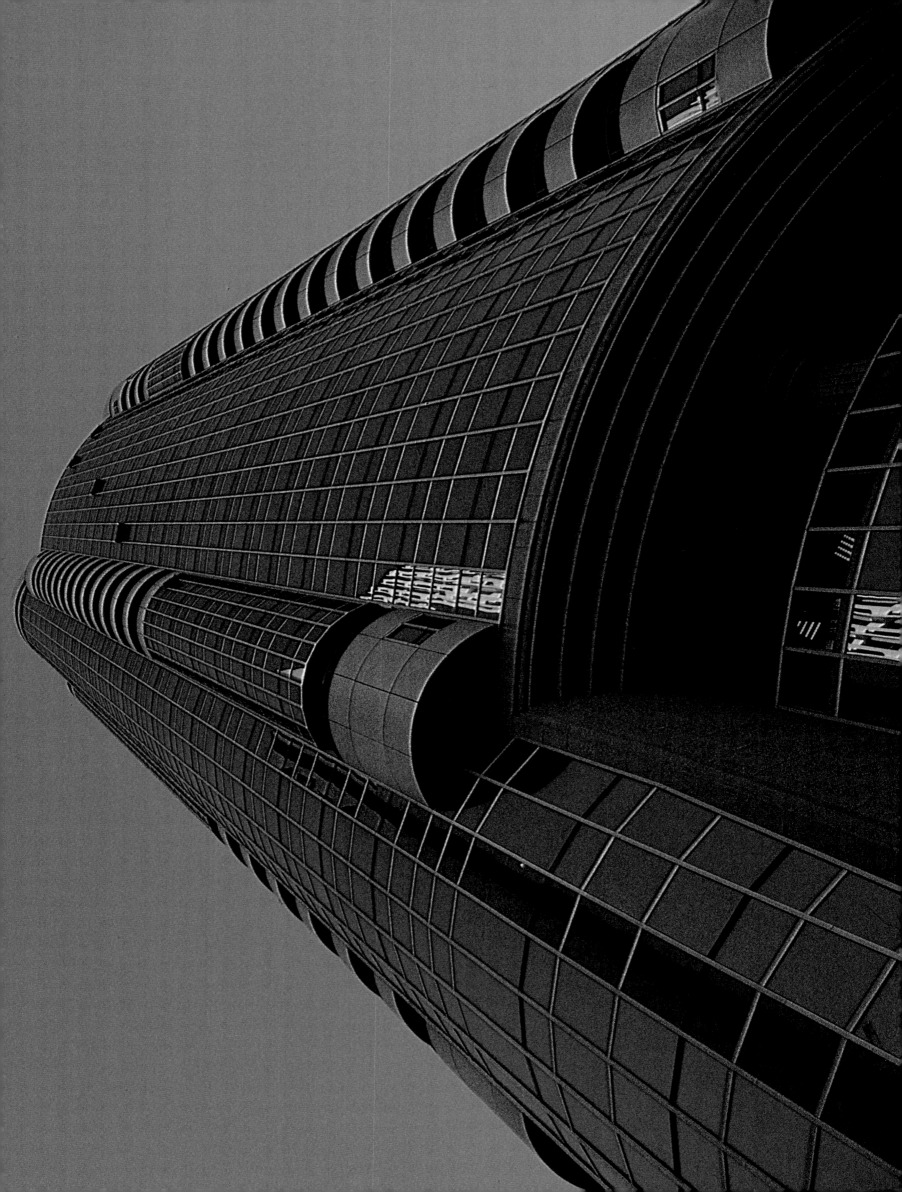

Antique Quran. Revealed to the Prophet Mohammad in the seventh century AD, the sacred text was originally committed to memory, and then written down on the shoulder-blades of camels and oxen. The introduction of bound paper texts like this one was a development which occurred only later. (*al-'Ain museum*)

RIGHT: Mosque with Ramadan moon, Abu Dhabi. Mosques in the Emirates were traditionally austere – often built of palm fronds, mud bricks or coral. Since 1971, however, more than two thousand new mosques have been constructed, many of them in monumental style.

PRECEDING PAGE: High-rise towers in the heart of Abu Dhabi. Forty years ago this was a sleepy village of coral and reed houses, whose most impressive building was a mud-brick fort. Today it is an array of glittering glass and concrete pinnacles of spectacular character and strikingly diverse design.

FOLLOWING PAGES

Etisalat telecommunications tower, Abu Dhabi. Its distinctive roof globe makes it an easily recognizable landmark. The globe is not for decoration only, but elegantly conceals powerful modern telecommunications equipment.

Etisalat Telecommunications tower, Dubai, built to exactly the same design and specifications as that in Abu Dhabi.

The Commercial Bank of Dubai in Abu Dhabi. An experimental combination of modern mirror glass with a traditional Islamic design, this building stands on the Corniche, and manages to capture the brilliant colours in the sunset so spectacularly that it seems to be illuminated from inside.

Dubai Chamber of Commerce and Industry, Dubai, by moonlight.

216

ABOVE: Shadowplay in Abu Dhabi's castle, reminiscent of ancient zigurats.

RIGHT: Sunrise above Battina, Abu Dhabi.

PRECEDING PAGE: View from the roof of a high-rise block, Abu Dhabi. Local architects have solved the problem of camouflaging unsightly lift-tackle and air-conditioning plant by the ingenious use of this wrought-iron grille with its elegant Islamic stellar design.

FOLLOWING PAGES

The Creek, Dubai, looking inland. Electric lights fire up as the night falls over the waterway controlled by the al-Maktoum family since 1833.

Water-taxis at work by Deira wharf, Dubai. Known as *'abaa'ir* [sing. *'abra*] such small boats have ferried passengers between the five parts of the town for several generations. Once rowed by hand, most are now motorized and carry many passengers.

View from the angled windows of the Dubai Chamber of Commerce, Dubai, overlooking the waterfront.

A little girl drawing, Abu Dhabi. This six-year-old girl (TOP) is so intent on her drawing that she has forgotten to join the other children on their break. When they return (CENTRE) she seems to feel that her artistic space has been invaded. She transfers herself to the floor (BOTTOM), where she continues, oblivious of anything beyond her work.

ABOVE: Boys in a classroom, Abu Dhabi. These schoolboys — aged ten — are among almost half a million students currently being educated in the schools, colleges and university of the United Arab Emirates, where the first modern educational establishment was built only in 1955.

BELOW: College students, Abu Dhabi. Thirty years ago, most literate people in the Emirates had been trained in traditional Quranic schools lit by oil lamps, in which students copied out verses from the Quran on the shoulder-blades of cattle. Today they study science and technology in cool, strip-lighted classrooms, with the benefit of calculators and overhead projector.

Artwork by schoolchildren in Abu Dhabi, aged from six to eleven years.

ABOVE: The techniques and spontaneous expression can be surprising. Here thick paint has been scratched with fingernails.

RIGHT: A lifesize figure of a man, draped naturalistically in real cloth.

Watchtower of Sharjah fort.

LEFT: The main fountain in Abu Dhabi.

PRECEDING PAGES: Dubai Creek Golf and Yacht Club, Dubai. The building, which displays resonances of the lateen-rigged Arab dhow, also has some of the features of the larger Sydney Opera House.

The serene domes and minarets of Sharjah's airport belie a busy international terminal.

RIGHT: Shadow of a helicopter over a marine delta, near Abu Dhabi.

FOLLOWING PAGES

The coastal waters of the Gulf are shallow, and during the greater part of the year the sun warms them up to a considerable temperature. Rapid evaporation makes for a continuously changing pattern of sandbanks, lagoons, and islands. Some of the larger ones are divided by miniature rivers, river deltas, inland seas. From the air these coastlines have a peculiar, inimitable beauty, and looking down one sees into one of the rare surviving nurseries of life on this planet.

The ancient medina of al-Shwaiheen, Sharjah. Some two hundred years ago this market place attracted traders who brought in their goods by caravanserai and sail from Europe, Asia and North Africa. The medina comprises several outstanding buildings, including the al-Arsa *souq*, now restored in one of the Emirates' largest and most successful attempts to return historic buildings to their original function. Outside the *madrasah*, a group of exotic-looking visitors should look out of place in the metropolitan heart of Sharjah. Here and at full moon they blend perfectly, answer to a photographer's prayer.

Watchtower, seen from the Maqta bridge, which was the first to link the island of Abu Dhabi with the mainland. In the background can be seen the lights of one of the Umm an-Nar petroleum refinery.

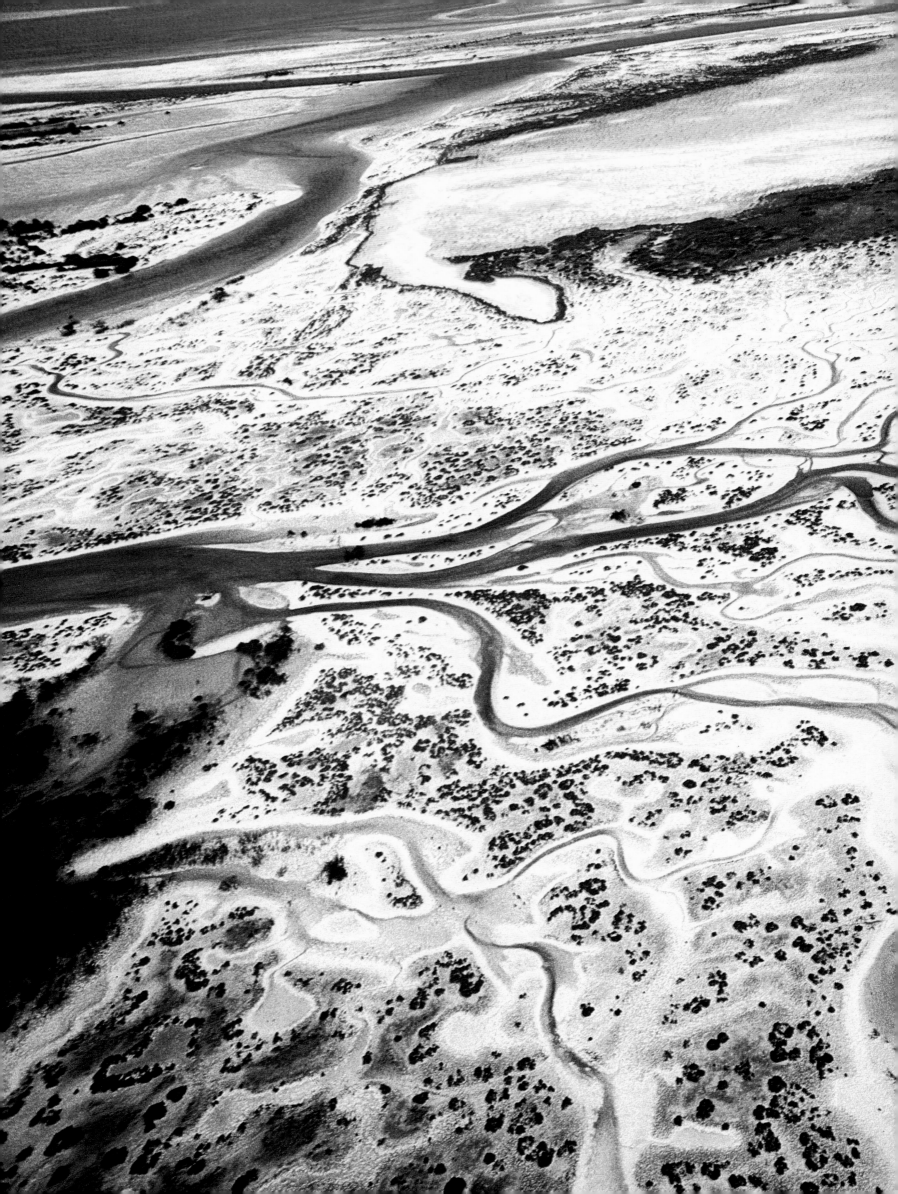

Water tower, Dubai. This elegantly designed, highly decorated reservoir has a capacity of 200,000 gallons per day and a through-flow capacity of two million gallons.

LEFT: Traditional well-mechanism, Abu Dhabi. This wooden frame, now reconstructed in Abu Dhabi's Heritage Village – a kind of living museum – was powered by camels or oxen, and employed a wooden wheel as a pulley to hoist up a leather well-bucket.

FOLLOWING PAGES

Communications relay station, Abu Dhabi Emirate. Sited in salt desert southwest of Abu Dhabi, one of a pair of Y-antennas has a built-in, computer-controlled power station which smoothly rotates the entire structure into the required position. The Y-arms can also be opened or folded depending on whether the transmission or receiving mode is required.

Ground station for sattelite communications – 'Earth Station'.

ACKNOWLEDGEMENTS

Phoenix Rising was made possible by the support and good will of HH Sheikh Mohammed bin Zayed and HH Sheikh Mansour bin Zayed al-Nahyan.

For their support and encouragement the publishers are grateful to Ibrahim al-Abed, to the Diwan of HH Sheikh Mohammed bin Rashid al-Maktoum, the good offices of Sheikh Hasher al-Maktoum and Sheikh Ahmed bin Sa'id al-Maktoum, Qasim Sultan, Easa al-Gurg, Mahdi al-Tajir, Yousef Omeir bin Yousef, Sultan bin Sulayem, Mohid-din Binhendi, Khalid bin Sulayem, Sultan al-Owais, Obaid al-Tayer, Juma al-Majid, Khalaf al-Habtoor, Ghazi al-Tajir, Abdallah al-Azdi, Nabil Zakhour, Sami Sidawi, Massoud Shahim, Mubarak bin Fahd, Peter Hellyer, Tamara Mufti, and to the many others who have made this project possible.

For permitting the photography included in this book the publishers gratefully acknowledge the following museums and collections: al-'Ain Museum; al-Fardan Jewellers and Precious Stones, Fujairah; Dubai National Museum; Fujairah Museum; The Juma Al Majid Center for Culture and Heritage, Dubai; National Museum of Ras al-Khaimah.

For their assistance at the time the photographs were taken, or subsequently with captions, the publishers acknowledge with gratitude the assistance of the following museum directors, curators, collectors, librarians and archaeologists: A. K. al-Shamsi, Director of Antiquities and Heritage, and Salah A. Hassan, Archaeologist, of the Fujairah Museum; Mustafa al-Fardan of al-Fardan Jewels & Precious Stones, Dubai; Jawad al-Moosawi, General Manager, of al-Fardan Arts and Jewellery Factory, Sharjah; Dr Walid Yasin, Archaeologist of al-'Ain Museum; Derek Kennet, Resident Archaeologist of the National Museum of Ras al-Khaimah; Mrs Ayesha Mubarak Abdallah Obeid, Head of Archaeology and Museums, of Dubai National Museum; Dr Abdal-Rahman Farfour of The Juma Al Majid Center for Culture and Heritage, Dubai; Sultan al-Owais, Dubai.

The publishers are grateful to Sir Wilfred Thesiger and Ronald Codrai for permission to reprint their photographs; and to Mr Hossein Amirsadeghi for his immeasurable contribution to the making of this book.

Cylinder seal and imprint from al-Sufouli, Umm an-Nar period, 2500–2000 BC. Carved in hard blueish stone. (*Dubai Museum*)